Nurture Through Nature

by Claire Warden

Mindstretchers™

Thank you...
To all the children who have shared their views on the world with us.
To all the early years environments around the world who have shared their visions and hopes.
To all our families for their patience and understanding over the last three years.
To all the creatures for giving their time freely and with real enthusiasm during photographic sessions.

Design and layout by Claire Warden and Jan Vickers 2007
Cover design by Almond www.almondtds.com +44 (0)131 553 5523
Printed by J. Thomson Colour Printers, Glasgow, UK

© Photography by Claire Warden & Nicki Buchan 2007

ISBN 978-1-906116-16-3

If you would like training materials or further information about the Fascination series, or any other Mindstretchers publication please contact:
enquiries@mindstretchers.co.uk

Glenruthven Mill
Abbey Road
Auchterarder
PH3 1DP
Scotland, UK

Tel: +44 (0)1764 664409
Fax: +44 (0)1764 660728
www.mindstretchers.co.uk
www.claire-warden.com

Foreword

The journey began three years ago with the birth of our third child and the awareness of the increasing speed of the passage of time. Born into a family who are firmly committed to being outside, she was able to connect to nature from a very early age. From the earliest point she has been able to let her opinions be known. She and her friends have been such inspiring teachers, that they deserve mention. The time to really connect to a small group of children does not happen every day, although it should. It is through communicating and connecting with very young children in natural spaces, that we have been able to bring you this book.

Contents

Introduction

This book will take you through the natural elements that underpin a human desire to connect and be 'in nature'. It is hoped that it will motivate and support you to consider the potential of an outdoor area for children under three and how you can respond to their motivations to create a magical natural environment full of awe and wonder.

I would love to share this book and this key photograph (opposite) with you to introduce you to an emotion that summarises the way that I see young children 'feel' when they are involved with nature. They are 'chuffed'! In a state of chuffedness, for the sheer joy of it all. We need to raise ourselves up a little to see naturalistic outdoor play in its simplest forms before we become too embroiled in the paper work and lose sight of what it is really all about.

There is a connection between the nurturing aspects of nature and human beings. Many people talk of calm places they go to when they need to think such as the beach, a forest, a park or an art gallery with images of nature. Through a process of watching children I have seen the way that they respond to a variety of environments and the response that staff have had. Phrases used such as "he changes when he has space", "It's that time... we need to take them out", "The baby will sleep well if you take her out in the pram". We have an underlying awareness of the need that children have for the fundamental aspects of being on the planet. It is these basic elements of nature that I have taken to structure this book. Nature is not always calm and soft, but it will always offer us the chance to learn about ourselves and

'Looking at the world from up on high'

the world around us. Nurture through nature is a way of looking at outdoor spaces and making choices about the types of provision we want for our children. The outdoor area has a special value, a place of space, changing light, temperature and sense. It is of no surprise therefore that it can fully engage children in a way that is wonderful to behold.

To that end the chapters are grouped around a natural element and the associated experiences that come from it. Children under three are constantly developing and shifting their understanding of the space they are in. In order to reflect this the case studies are learning stories. They are not activities presented to children but transformational play that can show how ideas evolve and connect in early childhood. The role of the adult is clearly defined in this process since in order to respond effectively we need to be able to understand what we are seeing, hearing

and experiencing. This book cannot go into detail about the methods of adult interaction, but suffice to say that it lies at the core of effective early years environments and especially in environments that rely on body language and oral understanding.

This book is designed to be read in conjunction with the other books that I have written. The 'Outdoor Play File' is a fully comprehensive file that details the issues surrounding the management of outdoor play, landscape features, seasonal ideas, and planning. The 'We-Go file' supports indoor and outdoor links in learning. 'The Right To Be Me' explores the rights that very young children have to high quality care. The 'Potential of a Puddle' details the core vision and values which are at the centre of the Early years Outdoor Play guidelines used across many regions in the United Kingdom and abroad to influence practice in their centres.

'Me clapping'

In this eighth book, I have taken the view of shared journeys to discover the elements of the natural outdoor environment for children under three.

This book follows the interests of a group of children aged between 6 months and 3 years old. The group seemed to be motivated by similar opportunities, many of which were revisited time and time again. It is these experiences that we have used in this book, with video footage, photographic evidence and observational notes we were able to follow the children's lead and observe how far they wanted to explore. The only limitation we used was real danger, and although listed was never reached by the children, since they all self assessed 'the physically tricky bits'.

If you are there now reading this book thinking to yourself that you don't have a babbling brook, or woodland glade the photographs are dedicated to you. We have worked in a range of spaces where children play; from a childminders garden, to a landscaped nursery, a square of safety surface attached to a door to a full nature kindergarten. Nature and skilful adults, who work with very young children in mind have created the images you can see of the landscape.

In our Nature Kindergarten in Perth and Kinross, Scotland, nature is the vehicle for our teaching and learning. We use a blend of three spaces, the natural indoor space, the outdoor environment and the wild wood. This enables the practitioners to create opportunities in nature that ensure progression in knowledge skills and attitude.

One of the group was exploring seeds and this naturally evolved into the exploration into sorting and quantity. The self-help environment enabled him to gather paper to record his thinking and additional resources that led to exploration of number shape. This interest extended into the outdoor area where he gathered seeds and sorted them onto pieces of bark that he found in the garden. During his time in the wild wood, he found fir cones and proceeded to balance them along the root of a tree. We are very lucky to have the three environments to work with, however most of our experiences can be transposed to more urban/sterile outdoor spaces. A great deal of our work is in spaces that offer challenges to practitioners and the children who play in them. One of the core elements is the relationship between adult, child and nature. This relationship creates a connection that can take place in any environment.

Our approach is highly consultative with all the children we meet, so we do hope that you hear their voices as you read this book.

The first chapter however belongs to you, the person, the human. Not the landscape, or an object, but to another human being who has it in their control to engage with these young children, to join them as a skilled participant in their world. Relationships and connections are what makes us, us. We depend on those people around us to give us feedback, to develop our attitudes and values. Young children are linked to the people around them; they want to create a bond, a relationship that is important to them.

So let us begin the journey. As part of that process we took on board our own development through reflection and thought in journals. If you have our Under Three Reflective Journal with this book we hope you enjoy it and would like to hear your thoughts as you create a journey of your own to develop outdoor experiences for the children that you know and care for.

Kind regards
Claire

Early Years Outdoors
Vision and Values for outdoor play

I have been involved in the creation of National Vision and Values. These are included here to support a consistent approach across the United Kingdom.

Vision and Values

The Vision for all young children

- All children have the right to experience and enjoy the essential and special nature of being outdoors from a very young age.

- Young children thrive and their minds and bodies develop best when they have free access to stimulating outdoor environments for learning through play and real experiences.

- Knowledgeable and enthusiastic adults are crucial to unlocking the potential of outdoors.

Core Values for high quality outdoor experiences for young children

1. Young children should be outdoors as much as indoors and need a well-designed, well-organised, integrated indoor-outdoor environment, preferably with indoors and outdoors available simultaneously.

2. Play is the most important activity for young children outside.

3. Outdoor provision can, and must, offer young children experiences which have a lot of meaning to them and are led by the child.

4. Young children need all the adults around them to understand why outdoor play provision is essential for them, and adults who are committed and able to make its potential available to them.

5. The outdoor space and curriculum must harness the special nature of the

outdoors, to offer children what the indoors cannot. This should be the focus for outdoor provision, complementing and extending provision indoors.

6. Outdoors should be a dynamic, flexible and versatile place where children can choose, create, change and be in charge of their play environment.

7. Young children must have a rich outdoor environment full of irresistible stimuli, contexts for play, exploration and talk, plenty of real experiences and contact with the natural world and with the community.

8. Young children should have long periods of time outside. They need to know that they can be outside every day, when they want to and that they can develop their ideas for play over time.

9. Young children need challenge and risk within a framework of security and safety. The outdoor environment lends itself to offering challenge, helping children learn how to be safe and to be aware of others.

10. Outdoor provision must support inclusion and meet the needs of individuals, offering a diverse range of play-based experiences. Young children should participate in decisions and actions affecting their outdoor play.

Rationale

We believe it is essential to underpin the Vision and in particular, the Values with a rationale for how this thinking came about, and more detailed information about what each Value means in reality. The additional details set out below reflect the thinking that took place and was recorded in the group sessions at the Vision and Values day on November 3rd 2003.

1. **Young children should be outdoors as much as indoors and need a well-designed, well-organised, integrated indoor-outdoor environment, preferably with indoors and outdoors available simultaneously.**

Outdoor provision is an essential part of the child's daily environment and life, not an option or an extra. Each half of the indoor-outdoor environment offers significantly different, but complementary experiences and ways of being for young children. They should be available simultaneously and be experienced in a joined-up way, with each being given equal status and attention for their contribution to young children's well-being, health, stimulation and all areas of development.

Outdoor space must be considered a necessary part of an early years environment, be well thought through and well organised to maximise its value and usability by children and adults, and design and planning must support developmentally appropriate practice, being driven by children's interests and needs.

2. Play is the most important activity for young children outside.

Play is the means through which children find stimulation, well-being and happiness, and is the means through which they grow physically, intellectually and emotionally. Play is the most important thing for children to do outside and the most relevant way of offering learning outdoors. The outdoor environment is very well suited to meeting children's needs for all types of play, building upon first-hand experiences.

3. Outdoor provision can, and must, offer young children experiences which have a lot of meaning to them and are led by the child.

Because of the freedom the outdoors offers to move on a large scale, to be active, noisy and messy and to use all their senses with their whole body, young children

engage in the way they most need to explore, make sense of life and express their feeling and ideas. Many young children relate much more strongly to learning that is offered outdoors rather than indoors.

All areas of learning must be offered through a wide range of holistic experiences, both active and calm, which make the most of what the outdoors has to offer.

Outdoor provision needs to be organised so that children are stimulated, and able, to follow their own interests and needs through play-based activity, giving them independence, self-organisation, participation and empowerment. The adult role is crucial in achieving this effectively.

4. Young children need all the adults around them to understand why outdoor play provision is essential for them, and adults who are committed and able to make its potential available to them.

Young children need practitioners who value and enjoy the outdoors themselves, see the potential and consequences it has for young children's well-being and development, and want to be outside with them. Attitude, understanding, commitment and positive thinking are important, as well as the skills to make the best use of what the outdoors has to offer and to effectively support child-led learning; the adult role outdoors must be as deeply considered as that indoors. Practitioners must be able to recognise, capture and share children's learning outdoors with parents and other people working with the child, so that they too become enthused. Cultural differences in attitude to the outdoors need to be understood and worked with sensitively to reach the best outcomes for children.

5. The outdoor space and curriculum must harness the special nature of the outdoors, to offer children what the indoors cannot. This should be the focus for outdoor provision, complementing and extending provision indoors.

The outdoors offers young children essential experiences vital to their well-being, health and development in all areas. Children who miss these experiences are significantly deprived.

Outdoors, children can have the freedom to explore different ways of 'being', feeling, behaving and interacting; they have space - physical (up as well as sideways), mental and emotional; they have room and permission to be active, interactive, messy, noisy and work on a large scale; they may feel less controlled by adults.

The real contact with the elements, seasons and the natural world, the range of perspectives, sensations and environments - multi-dimensional and multi-sensory, and the daily change, uncertainty, surprise and excitement all contribute to the desire young children have to be outside. It cannot be the same indoors, a child cannot *be* the same indoors - outdoors is a vital, special and deeply engaging place for young children.

'Self-help systems that offer natural, open-ended materials'

6.   Outdoors should be a dynamic, flexible and versatile place where children can choose, create, change and be in charge of their play environment.

Outdoor provision can, and should, offer young children an endlessly versatile, changeable and responsive environment for all types of play where they can manipulate, create, control and modify. This offers a huge sense of freedom, which is not readily available indoors. It also underpins the development of creativity and the dispositions for learning. The space itself as well as resources, layout, planning and routines all need to be versatile, open-ended and flexible to maximise their value to the child.

7.   Young children must have a rich outdoor environment full of irresistible stimuli, contexts for play, exploration and talk, plenty of real experiences and contact with the natural world and with the community.

Through outdoor play, young children can learn the skills of social interaction and friendship, care for living things and their environment, be curious and fascinated,

experience awe, wonder and joy and become 'lost in the experience'. They can satisfy their deep urge to explore, experiment and understand and become aware of their community and locality, thus developing a sense of connection to the physical, natural and human world.

A particular strength of outdoor provision is that it offers children many opportunities to experience the real world, have first-hand experiences, do real tasks and do what adults do, including being involved in the care of the outdoor space. Settings should make the most of this aspect, with connected play opportunities.

An aesthetic awareness of and emotional link to the non-constructed or controlled, multi-sensory and multi-dimensional natural world is a crucial component of human well-being, and increasingly absent in young children's lives. The richness of cultural diversity is an important part of our everyday world; this can and should be explored by children through outdoor experiences. Giving children a sense of belonging to something bigger than the immediate family or setting lays foundations for living as a community.

8. Young children should have long periods of time outside. They need to know that they can be outside every day, when they want to and that they can develop their ideas for play over time.

High quality play outdoors, where children are deeply involved, only emerges when they know they are not hurried. They need to have time to develop their use of spaces and resources and uninterrupted time to develop their play ideas, or to construct a place and then play in it or to get into problem-solving on a big scale. They need to be able to return to projects again and again until 'finished' with them.

Slow learning is good learning, giving time for assimilation. When children can move between indoors and outside, their play or explorations develop further still. Young children also need time (and places) to daydream, look on or simply relax outside.

9. Young children need challenge and risk within a framework of security and safety. The outdoor environment lends itself to offering challenge, helping children learn how to be safe and to be aware of others.

'Emotional space'

Children are seriously disadvantaged if they do not learn how to approach and manage physical and emotional risk. They can become either timid or reckless, or be unable to cope with consequences. Young children need to be able to set and meet their own challenges, become aware of their limits and push their abilities (at their own pace), be prepared to make mistakes, and experience the pleasure of feeling capable and competent. Challenge and its associated risk are vital for this. Young children also need to learn how to recognise and manage risk as life-skills, so as to become able to act safely, for themselves and others.

Safety of young children outdoors is paramount and a culture of 'risk assessment to enable' that permeates every aspect of outdoor provision is vital for all settings. Young children also need to feel secure, nurtured and valued outdoors. This includes clear behavioural boundaries (using rules to enable freedom), nurturing places and times outside and respect for how individual children prefer to play and learn.

10. Outdoor provision must support inclusion and meet the needs of individuals, offering a diverse range of play-based experiences. Young children should participate in decisions and actions affecting their outdoor play.

Provision for learning outdoors is responsive to the needs of very active learners, those who need sensory or language stimulation and those who need space away from others – it makes provision more inclusive and is a vital learning environment. When children's learning styles are valued, their self-image benefits. Boys, who tend to use active learning modes more than girls and until they are older, are particularly disadvantaged by limited outdoor play.

All children need full access to provision outdoors and it is important to know and meet the needs and interests of each child as an individual. Young children react differently to the spaces and experiences available or created so awareness and flexibility are key to the adult role. Observation and assessment (formative and summative), and intervention for particular support, must be carried out outside. While it is important to ensure the safety of all children, it is equally important to ensure all are sufficiently challenged.

Young children should take an active part in decisions and actions for outdoor provision, big and small. Their perspectives and views are critical and must be sought, and they can take an active role in setting up, clearing away and caring for the outdoor space.

Relationships

The Adult Role ..

The work we do is based on our underlying beliefs and values that underpin what we do every day so that all small decisions lead us in the right direction. These are the beliefs that we uphold as a team of adults, the process of their creation is the core to their effectiveness. In the Potential of a Puddle (Warden 2005) there is a section on policy writing and the same issues apply here. This is our policy and it is backed up by ways of working, so that any visitors or new team members can see how our work with the young children in our care allows them to explore curiosity, investigation and risk taking. Our commitment to care and affection is paramount to us and although most documents do mention it, its place is sometimes behind learning rather than integral to it. The balance of care and challenge is the key to enabling each and every child to develop their emotional intelligence and the belief in themselves. The Right to be Me (Warden 2002)

The quality of the outdoor play and therefore its potential as a space to support learning is clearly linked to the adults. Working with young children is all about relationships; their relationship with each other, a caring adult, or their inter- relationship with the spaces around them.

Adult interaction is the hardest aspect to teach in training, knowing when to be near, to offer space, or a challenge, seems to come from within a sensitive, knowledgeable adult.

The staff role in an outdoor learning environment is integral to its success. Although planning can be put into place, the environment organised, and the children present, it will be the ongoing commitment and enthusiasm of the staff to learning out of doors that will ensure its sustainability. McLean (1991) refers to the effective adult as going through a process of fine tuning on a continual basis. This describes the role well; to look at children, analyse their learning, respond to it whilst still maintaining a curricular background is one of the skills of being an early years facilitator.   The people we see that have this skill have developed a view of learning that takes it away from an inside space to a mobile, experiential process and are able to identify it in all its forms. (Warden 2006)

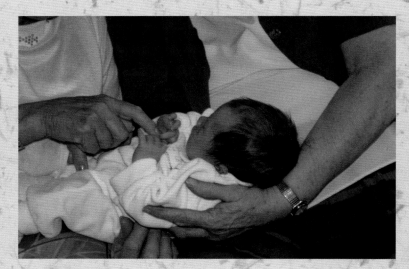

This fine tuning can involve the removal, or addition of resources to widen the play or to redirect it e.g. The provision of containers to carry sand in, a piece of rope to walk about with, a camouflage net to walk underneath. Deceptively simple opportunities often require complex thinking. It requires a perception to notice events and needs as they evolve. The toddler who appears to be wandering the outdoor area may actually be giving you a play cue that he needs a bag to add a focus to his drive for movement.

The issue of tidying up areas can often come in the way of learning, outdoor play is a creative process and as such generates mess. Muddy puddles, ropes, tyres to crawl under, and loose materials to transport are not seen to be learning resources to some adult eyes. The adult perception can be that materials designed by adults have a greater value. Adults who are knowledgeable about the way that young children learn can see beyond the plastic façade and see that beyond many of these resources lies limited exploration and learning.

Adults can offer children support to move out of their comfort zone, to feel and experience the outdoor space and then let go of the adult to explore on their own. Intrinsic motivation comes with personal rewards. The internal belief that children should be outside, will ensure that children are given the opportunity every day despite the weather. Obstructions to outdoor learning such as people who feel that 'babies are too fragile', 'toddlers should not eat dirt', 'their designer baby-grow will get dirty', 'new skin should be protected' are seen as opportunities for a discussion rather than reasons to give up. Our

perception of the environment and our feelings about a child's ability to cope affect the degree of experimentation and responsibility we allow them.

'Driving at 3 years old'

The two pictures of a 3 year old driving a speedboat in Sweden are testament to this. I have worked with young children for over 20 years and have had so many experiences of what they can achieve in risk-based play that I thought I was comfortable with risky play. However to be in a real position of 'trusting' a three year old with my life (or at least that was my perception!) was a thought provoking experience. Do we really trust them to make the right decision or do we play at it?

The 'Barnharge' in Norway have had a profound effect on the way we have set up our Whistlebrae Nature Kindergarten in Perthshire, in that they entrust very young children to be their own risk assessors.

The gender balance of under three staff teams is towards female dominance which carries with it some of the stereotypical roles of our society. Females are becoming more focused on outdoor play and learning although many do not find it a natural place to work. Tizard (1977) found that there were significant differences in the way staff worked indoors and out of doors. The interaction and cognitive challenges in some instances was lower out of doors, whereas the 'safety type' of interaction of 'don't go on the slope' increased. Many staff working with children under three have benefited from outdoor waterproof leggings so that they can sit in the mud or jump in the puddles along with the babies and toddlers in their care.

It is important in any team to create a joint belief system so that the values of the centre are maintained by all. We have chosen a shape from nature to share our core beliefs. The way in which the shapes fit together mimics the honeycombed nature of life. There are a number of curriculum documents that are used to guide practitioners working with young children. Although we refer to these, our programme for younger children is more based on tenderness, nearness and affirmation.

We let them try, try, try.

The child should feel good enough and not be limited by adult expectations

We give a feeling of safety and warmth.

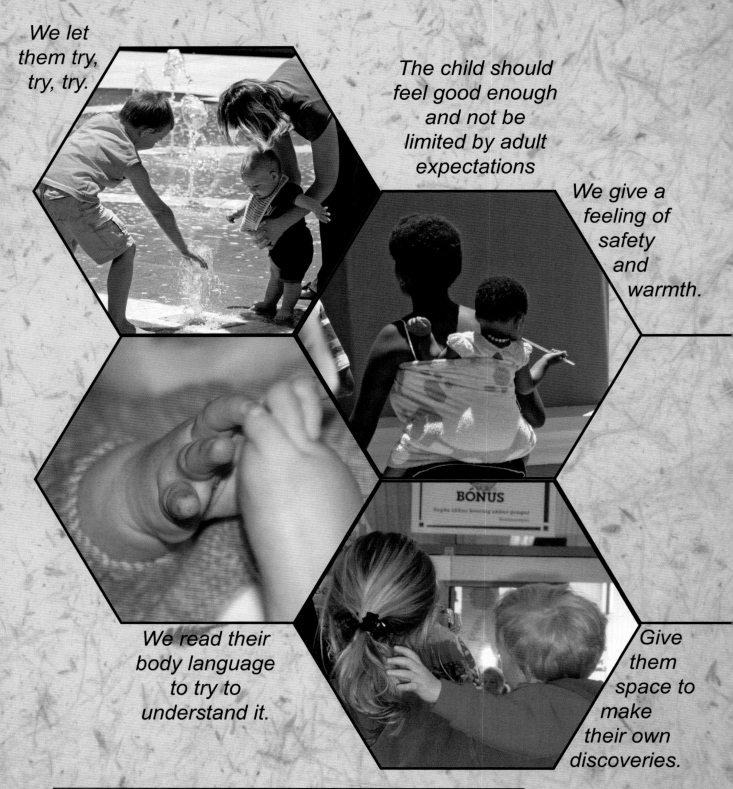

We read their body language to try to understand it.

Give them space to make their own discoveries.

Every child should reach a maximum development in their own time.

We give them activity which gives them mobility.

We talk about feelings and caring for each other.

We listen very carefully and try to understand their thoughts.

Together with parents we create harmonious children.

Sustainable projects and methods of working are obviously the most beneficial. There are numerous establishments that have created outdoor areas through the motivation of one /two key people. When these key people move on it is possible to see areas decline in both their use and maintenance. The development of a way of working that supports the community that the children come from, their carers and of course the centre will become embedded in practice. The case study element here explores the creation of 'Out and About' Home link ideas to encourage natural outdoor connections. The programme is based on schemas using natural elements. These are presented in a way that they become memories of learning that create links across discreet curriculum areas. The curriculum subjects are therefore woven throughout all the hip-pouches that we provide. Some of the ideas we have used are given below, feedback from parents has always been very positive.

Take a friend to meet a tree, walk around it getting to know it.

Made mud soup or chocolate milkshake in a puddle.

Find a leaf and peep through it (make a tube or a hole).

Lets go for a walk and collect stones. Then go back and try to remember where they came from.

Can you take a dead stick apart and put it back together ?

How may times can you wrap up a stone or a stick ?

Mud

The sensorial feeling of playing in mud and with soil is something that many people explore throughout their lives. As gardeners everywhere take off their gloves because 'It doesn't feel right' we should all consider how important it is for young children to be exposed to dirt. In a world where designer clothing and largely unfounded fears about the hidden germs in dirt abound, there is a need to consider the long term effect of 'too much' hygiene.

Children in their teens are being exposed for the first time to germs and bugs that they should have encountered in childhood where they have the increased ability to produce more antibodies. When a group of children were monitored by parents at the Norwegian Barnharge, the incidence of colds and infections actually went down as the time they spent outside increased (Oslo University 2005).

There are considerations about the access that children have to soil and mud if cats, dogs and wildlife use the area. If we believe that children should have access to mud and soil then we can do a number of things to support this access whilst still considering health issues. The area can be planted with non-irritant/non-poisonous plants that crawling babies and toddlers can have access to. Create smaller sand areas with tyres, wooden edging that can have a lid or a cover.

If we look at how mud and sand are naturally presented to us it is often I large banks or isolated patches between two rocks. It was watching some toddlers dip their fingers into these tiny natural bowls that created the 'boulder cups'. These boulders are rounded with artificial dips and hollows created on the sides and top, to encourage young to explore with their fingers.

Some centres have gone so far as to sterilise soil by micro-waving tubs of it for small-scale experiences for very young children. There is a move in an area in Japan to create whole indoor outdoor play areas for young children. One of the attractions for parents is a policy of fumigation that will sterilise the area once a week. In a culture that has a very high emphasis on cleanliness and hygiene it seems to support the culture of the family, but one does wonder what the long-term effect of this provision will be on the resistance of the teenagers and adults.

In the learning story below a group of children were attracted by an outdoor truck in a wilder area of the outdoor play zone. It shows very clearly the nature of transformational play and how the key element of an effective outdoor play area is an adult to facilitate the opportunities through time and to a certain extent resources.

The soil was dry and the children were putting handfuls into the truck. The cantilever action of the back of the truck interested the children and the negotiation between one child putting it under the back area and

'Transporting dirt'

those wanting to put it in the truck took some time.

As the more dominant child took the lead the second child moved towards another container in the shape of a leaf. Taking the same soil she sprinkled it into the leaf where it was immediately immersed into a small amount of water that was at the base. The disappearance of the soil stimulated the need for more handfuls of soil until a small amount was left at the top, in order to make it disappear the child picked up a stick to push it around. The rotation of the stick became the schema she was interested in. More water was added to the mixture and then more soil. The mud began to overflow onto the concrete. Since the base of the leaf was unstable it was impossible to keep all the liquid in. The water flowed out of the leaf and became a pool of water on the hard surface. Her interest transformed into the use of her fingers to pull out lines from the muddy puddle exploring

'Filling and emptying trailers'

'Mud soup'

the lines, textures, and temperature of the cold water. When her fingers became a little cold she reached for a stick and used this as the tool to draw the water mud out. The adult made a simple question of 'Are you painting?' and placed some brushes near by. The brushes were noticed straight away but rather than drawing from the mud with sticks she got a container and filled it with water mud and then used it like a paint pot on the floor.

'Mud stew'

After several minutes she went to an area where there are some old tiles and carried one back to the wild area where she drew on it like a piece of paper.

The tile became a favourite possession and was carried around the area for the rest of the session. A simple affirming statement can re-direct play to be more structured than intended. The little girl was painting in 'her way' and changed her behaviour to ' paint' in the way associated with the adults.

In the next series of play sessions resources such as different tile sizes and shapes, a variety of thick brushes and sticks of varying diameters were offered.

This learning story shows imaginative mud play emerging and developing when the two year old girl watches and copies an older child playing outdoors. The little girl

was able to fill her bucket from the water dispenser. She repeatedly filled and emptied her bucket, pouring the water onto the ground next to the water dispenser until she stood in a muddy puddle, she stamped in the mud and continued to fill and empty her bucket. An older boy collected water and she followed the boy. She stood and watched him add leaves, mud and sticks to his water and stir it as he made mud-soup with his friend. She took her bucket, collected more water and sat down to add leaves.

"I make soup" she said as she added soil and stirred the mixture with her stick. "You want soup?" The following day she showed her 2 year old friend how to make mud soup. "Look, mine brown. Yours brown too" "You need more mud?" "Mine hard, look my stick muddy!" "I make mud-soup" "I make chocolate soup". They experimented adding more sticks and leaves and then removing them as stirring became more difficult.

"I make hot chocolate" said one and took her bucket to the pretend fire where the older children had been playing. Both hung their buckets over the fire and stood back to watch.

'Mud and Soil' resources

Miniature buckets
trowels
Forks
Rakes
Buckets in a variety of sizes and types
Garden trug
Dibber
Short lengths of broom handle or sticks for
creating holes
Plastic animals such a moles beetles
and bugs to hide
A variety of sizes of plant pots and labels
Watering can
Large cauldrons and giant spoons
A puddle
Mud
Access to giant leaves to use as plates
Pieces of bark for trays
Loose material to add to the soup

Sand has always had a fascination for children from the earliest memories of days on the beach, to gritty sandwiches and watching toes disappear into soft wet sand. Some people love it and others suffer it! Young children engage in it fully using all their senses to explore it. Sandy beaches are on offer to some of our children in the United Kingdom who live on the coast and have a beach for a playground. For the rest of the population who work with young children we need to consider the material itself, how children use it and therefore how we support their curiosity and present it to them in interesting ways.

'Reassurance and support'

This 11 month old baby was walking on a beach between her mother and

grandmother. She lifted her feet up high walking as she walked on the warm, dry and soft sand. The texture of the sand gradually changed as they approached the water and the sand became damp and more solid under her feet. Due to

the variable nature of sand and water mixing together subtle changes in the pressure under the child's foot will have sent strong messages to cerebellum. She walked into the water where she could feel the cool waves

gently lapping over her feet. She then sat down in the deeper water where she enjoyed the sensorial experience of the sandy, salty waves washing over her whole body stimulating all her senses.

Since the whole body is gathering information and feeding it back to the brain, young children should be able to use that aptitude by feeling and experiencing materials with all their senses in their hands, feet and body. The sand areas featured in this section vary

from whole beach areas to large outdoor sandpits, sand sheds and then onto smaller tuff trays and trays on the floor. The indoor experiences are more controlled and discrete, although one nursery I had the pleasure of visiting in England had a sunken sandpit with decking in the toddler room.

The sand itself can be of a variety of types to create different experiences. Soft rounded sand or silver sand is so very fine that when it is dry it flows through wheels and mechanisms as if it is water.

Builders sand has a degree of grit within it which means that it holds shapes and structures effectively. The builders sand we have it wonderful for outdoor play since the rain can effectively sieve the sand leaving piles of small stones on the top surface that are often collected as a form of treasure by the 2 year olds and put into small buckets to transport around the outdoor area.

Sands can be bought/found in a variety of colours and used as a palette of colour in outdoor spaces. Older children use it to create patterns, whilst younger children enjoy the stimulation of colour and interaction with a pliable material that changes each time they visit it. In challenging spaces that are small, and often rather limited in natural provision of resources, small amounts of a variety of sands can be offered in a treasure basket type experience for babies. Some centres already have indoor heuristic play sessions for the babies and toddlers, but could do a lot more about outdoor heuristic play so that the babies also experience wind, rain and light and shadow.

The provision of water and any sand creates a completely new material. A shallow tuff tray with a small amount of sand and a puddle of water create far more opportunities for play that either material on their own. My approach to landscape would be that children should play in an outdoor spaces where running water, sand and rocks combine in

a naturalistic way. So that young children see the effect of water on the dry rocks, hear babbling water over rocks and then its silence over sand. Nature offers all the best ideas and for landscape design for children we should look at the juxtaposition of materials and surfaces to create natural connections I their play spaces. Some centres have created enclosed pebble pool bases with large upstanding boulders that dribble water over the area.

The sand will damage most pumps so the area has to be enclosed or perhaps created with a sandy rock and then surrounded by large flat stones. The simplest way to combine them is to explore the possibilities of a rain butt that collects from down pipes and is set on a large sand pit. Large sand areas are a delight to children but they do seem to offer adults a challenge, many see urban foxes and cats as deterrents, we can build in raking as part of the closing down of the area and then see clearly who has visited the area and where they have been. Any sand can then be removed.

Toni and Robyn Christi who are based in Wellington, New Zealand have created mud/ soil enclosures with simple shade roof and planking walls with narrow gaps or Perspex

insets so that the light can get in. Through using a drop down canvas on the front that can be rolled back during play the usable space has been maximised.

Sand provides an open-ended resource that can be used in an endless variety of ways. Children can explore the way it moves, they transport it wet and let it flow when dry. They can create new potions and

'Learning from each other'

soups on a daily basis. Children can create sludgy places when it is wet and a warm tickly place when dry. Children will lie in it, roll over it, cover their legs with it and enjoy the moment when they rediscover their toes. Sand can hide things very quickly and then allow children to feel around to find them again. It can be shaped into tall towers, low bowls and dips to hide in, sand walls to lean against and mounds to jump on and over. Wet sand can be used to make light patterns in the winter time by

putting tealights into shallow dips and watching them flicker outside or from a near by window.

The approach of observing behaviours called schemas is outlined at the back of the book. Children often engage in the behaviours listed above but then go on to extend their ideas along a similar track of interest. Enclosing and enveloping can explain the connection that children have between hiding a ball, a rock, a jewel, or toes underneath the sand. Their enjoyment of

repeating the idea with slightly different resources, shows their fascination with the behaviour rather than it being a single activity. The schema section at the back of this book explains the features of schema and how we can see the behaviours in outdoor play areas, the simple activities that young children enjoy are often complex to them, packed full of investigation, curiosity and intrigue.

The learning story here takes place in a nursery that has recently transformed their

playground into a wonderful place for children to play and explore. One corner of the playground has been edged with some large logs. These provide support for a variety of behaviours. They are used to lean against, pull up, sit astride and to crawl along. In order to support the babies so that they can be fully immersed in the area the sand is in a large area. And connects over the log to a sensory area with herbs, sandy loam soil and flat areas. One of the children saw a bucket in the corner and made his way over to it. When he arrived he took everything out of the bucket and proceeded to empty and fill the tubes and connectors. He tried to lift the sand but could not do it as effectively as the plastic object, so he returned to the black tubes. After some time he moved over the log and into the muddier area where he made a move to get a stone. The two surfaces and types of loose material enabled the baby to experience the textures of not only the objects he handled, but also the sensation of gross motor movement over the ground surfaces. The process of putting the body into a place of disequilibria builds up the neural pathways in the child's brain that develops gross motor capabilities. A variety of surfaces should be provided for young children and are explored in the landscape section.

'Sand' resources

Grit
Coarse sand
Builders sand
Silver sand
White sand
Beach sand (bits of broken shell)
Play sand
Black sand

Sand changes the way it behaves when it is combined with water and other natural resources such as water and wood so combinations of materials will engage young children for longer blocks of time.

Children use all their senses when they explore natural materials, so provide sand in a way that allows children to get into it:-
Low containers
Plastic sheets
Tuff trays
Flowerpots
Gravel trays
Long thin trays
Climb in sandpits with covers for shade and protection
A sand shed.
On a beach!

Stones

The core of the earth is molten stone – everything that we do is affected by the magnetism it creates so it is no surprise that human beings are so linked to rocks and the shapes they create. Children enjoy handling rocks of all shapes and sizes, marveling at their awe and wonder. As adults some of us have lost the ability to see the special beauty of Nature. These young children have only been on the planet for a few years so the shape of a stone fascinates them, the texture inspires them, the appearance of sparkles and glints amaze them because they are meeting these simple materials for the first time.

Collections of smooth rocks in a basket can be cleaned for a baby zone; pebbles can be embedded into panels or smooth areas to create a textural surface to crawl over.

Large smoothed boulders offer natural 'pull-ups' for those children who are ready to be vertical. Lower rocks with rounded shapes offer a platform to crawl onto and

'Attempting to lift a rock'

explore. Small hollows over the surface can be used to create tiny bowls of water/leaves to investigate.

As part of the risk assessment we need to be aware of the children that we have and how much support they need. Children are natural explorers and I believe that they move to objects and areas that interest them.

'Investigating smaller stones that can be uplifted'

'Sitting in stones'

Eleanor Goldenschmid introduced the idea of babies using real objects to explore – some of these heuristic materials used were stones. Stones for babies are presented in the treasure basket – as the children become more mobile bags of materials are hung in a quiet space, free from distraction for children to explore. These experiences should continue for 2 years plus and some should be available throughout the session. Present the stones in mixed shape groups with woven baskets or offer similar shapes to create

experiences of circularity, texture etc. Create a wide range of types to encourage sensory exploration.

'Mark-making with stones'

The beauty of many stones can be accentuated by water – paintbrushes with water will always be essential to young children as they explore changes in colour and shade. Offer shallow bowls of smooth rocks so that the upper surface is dry and light while the lower surface is wet and dark. Opportunities to mark-make on rocks offer a great deal of

'Exploring walls and rocks'

potential for science as young children naturally try to find a small stone that will be effective. This exploration and fascination with stone and rock starts

from a very young age. In some centres which are troubled by urban foxes part of the risk assessment may involved washing rocks in baby zones.

In centres where there is little option but total safety surface we provide stone mats – designed for tile insets - to offer babies and toddlers the experience as a temporary solution.

Digging to find something or digging just for the joy of digging is motivational as soon as children are able to control their movements enough to direct their actions. Grasping bits of soil or

stone moves into the use of tools to make the process of discovery more effective. The sequence of photographs show the exploration of soil and stones presented in a cruising wall. These walls are detailed in the landscaping section and offer a way of presenting soil, stones and vegetation in flat landscapes.

The girl moved large leaves and then moved the grass aside to reach the soil surface. Once there she used her fingers to poke a hole into the soil. She repeated this several times, eventually discovering something hard just below the surface. When she had found the stone, she proceeded to excavate around it pulling aside more grass and soil to uncover the smooth stone. When she found the stone and was able to lift it out her facial expression was one of pleasure and achievement. She continued and found a second more angular stone. To explore the stone she put it in her mouth, rejected it and then put it back into the trough.

Consultation lies at the root of the work I do with young children. The ability and skill to interact with and consult a two year old, actually requires great skill and patience. The desire to have your thinking acknowledged starts from a very young age. The Talking and Thinking Floorbooks are designed to create a community of learning. This enables all children to revisit their learning by hearing their ideas read back or by looking at photographs of themselves engaged in play. The photograph (top right) was taken of a floorbook, stimulated by an interest in rocks. The child in the photograph started to make small marks on the rocks and then went on to:

'Investigating rocks in a Talking & Thinking Floorbook'

- Draw around them
- Wrap them up
- Wash them
- Put them in her pocket
- Take them for a walk
- Sing to them
- Hide them under a cloth
- Carry them around the area and back to the book
- Filled handbags with them
- Lined them up
- Jumped around them
- And finally put them in a puddle outside.

'Talking to a friend'

Many adults may view an interest in stone to be rather limiting and yet through the work I do with children I am constantly amazed by the creativity and curiosity displayed by young children when they are offered the opportunity to really engage and connect with stones and rock.

Look at our stones.
(Brendon)

11.04.2006

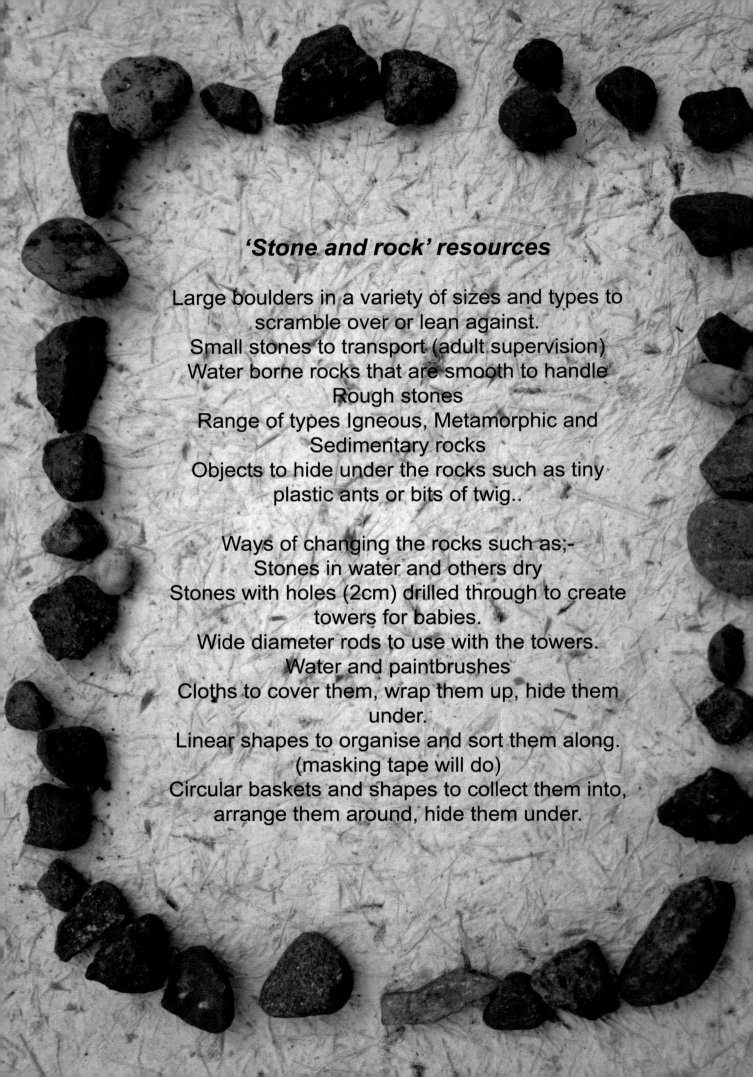

'Stone and rock' resources

Large boulders in a variety of sizes and types to
scramble over or lean against.
Small stones to transport (adult supervision)
Water borne rocks that are smooth to handle
Rough stones
Range of types Igneous, Metamorphic and
Sedimentary rocks
Objects to hide under the rocks such as tiny
plastic ants or bits of twig..

Ways of changing the rocks such as;-
Stones in water and others dry
Stones with holes (2cm) drilled through to create
towers for babies.
Wide diameter rods to use with the towers.
Water and paintbrushes
Cloths to cover them, wrap them up, hide them
under.
Linear shapes to organise and sort them along.
(masking tape will do)
Circular baskets and shapes to collect them into,
arrange them around, hide them under.

Water

Water is at the root of all life; without it we cannot survive and as such it connects to us in a root way. Outdoor play should allow children to be surrounded by water based experiences from jumping in a puddle, to hearing it trickle over stones.

Water can be presented on a large scale or a small one depending on the landscape.

'Anticipation'

It can be in natural spaces such as puddles or in manufactured shapes such as a tray. The nature kindergarten at Whistlebrae has access to a shallow rill which provides endless opportunities to explore natural spaces. The puddles on the way to the rill are of key importance and are enjoyed by adults and children every day.

Discussions move around their size, shape, depth and surface. We suggest songs to sing and rhymes to share. The youngest members of our group wonder at the disappearance of their wellington boots and the movement of the chocolate brown water. We laugh and giggle at funny puddle dances we can do.
The children we worked with engaged fully in the water zone. The babies responded to sound and visual stimulation through the reflection and light.

'Result'

'Wonderment as the water is displaced'

Nurture Through Nature

The older children were fully engaged with the water, if it was placed in a low bowl , they not only touched it but soon began to show signs of wanting to be fully immersed in the process. The hand went in the bowl, then the arm, then the leg and then the whole body, no matter how small the container. The only answer to water play is full romper suits or the potential to go to swimwear or total basics!

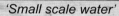

'Small scale water'

The landscape we offer children is part of the development of outdoor learning. The adult and child relationship unlocks its potential. With basic natural provision children will play and the adult develops that by giving them the supportive relationship to try.

'Large scale water'

Environmental awareness has to be at the core of our work so that we reuse water from the play bowls on the vegetation, water used for transporting is collected in sealed rain butts that are monitored and cleaned at regular intervals. Through the provision of a

tap young children are able to develop their independence.   Warm water offers longer term water play on colder days, since small fingers chill very quickly.

Many countries provide shallow paddling pools for the children inside centres throughout the year. They range from purpose built shallow hollows to inflatable commercial paddling pools.

The following learning story was full of transformational play and problem solving. One advantage of living in a wet climate is that we have a lot of water so a slow flowing trickle of water is possible.

The hose pipe was in the decking area and was combined with plastic bottles with a variety of neck size to offer some challenge. Trying to put the water in the bottle was

the greatest engagement. The bottle was put on the top of the hose, then put underneath to catch the dribbles running down the hose. After changing hands the bottle went into the left hand and the hose in the right she put the hose head on top of the bottle. The interest in the water coming out transferred to the water going back into the hosepipe. The girl took the bottle of water and started to refill the hosepipe. The

position of the bottle and the hose were altered several times until finally the water was allowed to come out of the hose into the bottle. After several minutes the bottle was put on the floor and the water dribbled from about a metre above. The hand and eye co-ordination was challenged as the water spout was irregular in shape and flow. Putting the bottle on a stool raised it up closer to the hose head. After spending 10 minutes filling the bottle and watching it overflow she then picked it up and emptied it out into a metal container. As the play moved forward away an adult put a small light ball into the container which re-ignited the interest. The water was dribbled into the container generally and then aimed again to hit the top of the ball. After filling the container several times the play moved away from the water area.

The next day the first area selected was the water zone. In response to the interest the day before the hose was set to a gentle dribble and put into a shallow tray with objects to target such as large stones. Similar behaviours were noticed of wanting to put the water on top of the stones, aiming to each in turn.

Later in the same session a second child transported some pegs over to the water. The little girl used the water hose to splash each one in turn. When the water was filling up the pegs started to move as they became caught in the motion of the water. The movement of the water began to overtake the target shooting. The adult responded by placing a basket of lightweight objects in the area. The leaves, feathers and corks soon became part of the water maelstrom as a group of children engaged around the large shallow tray to watch the water swirl the objects around.

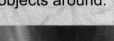

'Water' resources

We can offer water experiences in a variety of ways that
are suitable for children under three.

Tuff trays offer a large shallow puddle that
can be used if you do not have a
playground that lacks the surprise element
of a puddle or two.
Water in a rill so that children can walk crawl
and sit in the water.
Water that flows in response to an action
such as a pump, switch etc. so that
children make a link between cause and effect.
Water that is presented in interesting
containers, some with lids others without.
Bowls of water changed with scents, rose
petals floating in it, lavender floating on
the surface, blue water (dyed with
vegetable dyes so that young children can eat it
safely).
Water that has a texture such as the
petals, vegetable slices.
Objects to use to stir and move the water.
Moving water such as fountains, sprays and jets,
and dribbles Wellie sprays. These are low level jets
of water that come out from holes in a hosepipe mounted
along a wall at a low level (10 cm above
the floor) when the water is on fine jets of water clean
Wellington boots. When using them with young children
the jets of water take over from the cleaning activity!

Snow and Ice

The environment that surrounds your centre has a real affect in terms of the climate of support but also in terms of the world climatic zone that it exists within. The nature of play outside is bound to be affected by the weather and temperature. In Scotland, we are fortunate to be in an area where we can rely on some snow arriving each winter. However in southern England the chance becomes more unlikely.

'Creating snow

Someone once told me that we calculate our age in snow years which is calculated by the number of winters that have seen snow. For some adults they have only seen minimal snow and the enthusiasm and concern about it are often affected by this. It is the one type of weather that is guaranteed to affect all the family from 2 to 92.

There are some children who will never have seen or been aware of snow. Consider what it would be like not to be able to go and play in something that is so rare as to only arrive 2 or 3 times a year. The wonderment of snow, of it falling, catching snow flakes on your tongue and making snow shapes is apparent in some adults as they join young children in their exploration. The issue around snow is that it is not frequent and so we are often not well equipped for it. In the Scandanavian countries the whole culture invests in equipment such as snow suits for day to day living. In the U.K., many people look at the expense of thermal boots, waterproof gloves, thermal suits for babies, fleece rompers for toddlers and consider it too much. I would suggest that even if we do not have long blocks of lying snow (around we do have colder days where it is often too cold to snow (around – 2 degrees), or days where the wind chill takes the actual temperature down to

'Making friends with a snowblob'

– 4 degrees. Although young babies are recumbent and the lack of mobility can bring issues about circulation through the extremities, there are thermal bags on the market, babies can sleep in cold air if their bodies and heads are warm.

The case study below shows how much learning often comes through a very short block of time. To prevent young children from going out in the snow, even for short blocks of time, is really limiting their opportunity for exploration and the consequent learning they might have had.

'Pushing into snow'

The children had been enjoying looking into holes, peering through holes in wood and spying through the gaps in the tree, hedge and fence. Their creativity explored going round on the paper and making holes in the paper with the brush. The snow fell and group of two and a half year olds were watching it fall. The children had access to sticks and carried forward their interest in holes by making holes in the thick drift

'Climbing on giant snowballs'

layers around the edge of the outdoor area. The adult suggested making balls and the children joined her, when they had made the balls they proceeded to make holes through them. An older child was called over to use his stronger stick, to go all the way through. The creation of a hole flowed into a sphere and back to holes. The schema linking them could well be circularity and it was this that the adult supported by the offering of stainless steel balls, snowballs, guttering for the snowballs, and the process of creating giant balls to climb on.

The interest in holes stayed with the group after the snow disappeared so that holes in trees, a stump with a bowl in the top, holes in leaves continued to be of interest.

The ice is fascinating and objects stuck into ice always create surprise and delight. The children ranged from 2-5 in a mixed age range. The younger children discovered that the drinking barrel outside had frozen and the children realised that there was an icicle hanging from the tap. The older child took off the lid and looked in to see the frozen scene. With adult the children all looked inside and took bits out to explore. One of the group enjoyed tasting and experiencing new materials by using her mouth. The interest in the snow was to eat it, and to suck the collar of her waterproof. The ice was licked, sucked and explored generally.

'Eating white snow'

The children were all vocal about the ice in discussions, each child using their motivation to talk about it…."it was hard and then it was soft".."I smashed it", "It was on my nose and I got cold" "this (tongue) is tingly now"

The rarity of ice always makes it full of wonderment. The ice in the water tray had appeared over night much to the delight of the children. The children tipped the ice out and it smashed. The then looked

through the pieces and talked about the way the world had gone 'wibbly'.   The circularity of the bowl created a discussion about the ice falling apart and what shape was it when it was whole.   The adults and children then proceeded to lay out the slices of ice to recreate a circular shape. ' Children shared their achievement through squeals of delight, 'I fix it', ' look at me, here it is', 'I made a big sweetie'. The play moved on to explore the slices of ice. They made towers of the thick slices and tried to balance them. They put them in rows, stood them on end to make pretend ice caves and dens for the polar bears. Some children picked the ice up in a bucket and walked around the area, one or two added water to the bucket and were surprised to see it float 'like a little shiny boat'. Several children used them to make marks on the wooden structures like a pen.

The children were outside experiencing the ice and snow and the changes this brought to their environment. One little girl was very reluctant to walk on the wooden walkway but watching her friends she cautiously followed them. She was very hesitant about stepping onto the slippery wobbly bridge but once having done it with adult support she was very proud that she could now do it. " I did it, I did it" The next day her friends were standing in the middle of the bridge, holding onto the rope and jumping up and down to make it move. She was keen to join her friends, asked them to stop jumping and used her experience and knowledge of the previous day to move to them. They jumped with her and she laughed. She saw the bigger boys running towards her and left the bridge. The boys ran over the bridge making it really shake and wobble. She stood watching her friends enjoy the experience of the wildly swinging bridge and again made her way to the centre of the bridge to

join them. She held on tightly and laughed out loud when the boys ran past her

– a major achievement for this initially scared and hesitant little girl. The staff had allowed children to do their own risk assessment with adult support and use the icy and slippery equipment in the garden to learn about the changes in nature.

'Snow and ice' resources

Rubber ice cubes trays various
Shallow shapes for the water to freeze in
Ice shapes
Coloured ice in large blocks
Flowers embedded in ice
Sticks and stones embedded in ice.
Objects half in and half out of the ice

Objects such as old flower heads/grasses/
branches for the snow to settle on.
Snow to roll in
Snow to taste on your tongue
Black cloths to store in the freezer to catch
snowflakes

Objects to use with the snow and ice trays
Brushes of a wide range of type and size

Metal

The sound and feel of running a stick along a fence is firmly placed in childhood memories. Metal has a different sound that can be incorporated into experiences with more natural materials to enrich experiences for children.

Giant bells

The experiences for older children may well include observations of the changes in different types of metal. With very young children who are mouthing I do use stainless steel for its inert qualities whilst still giving wonderful auditory opportunities.

The photograph was taken in Iceland in an area designed for two year olds. The sand is volcanic and therefore black. Children spend long blocks of time outside each day and were encouraged to self-assess risk.

A group of 3 boys aged 2 years found some sticks on the far side of the outdoor area. The play started by drumming on the side of the wooden house, after 10 minutes of this exploration the boys split up and started to hit other objects. One found that the fence made a harder, louder noise. The noise attracted the other boys to the area. They played on the fence for several minutes before carrying on their journey around the area. As part of that exploration they walked along a wooden platform in the eaves of the shelter. The sides of the hut are faced with corrugated iron panels. Using the same sticks the boys moved along the walkway alternating walking and running. By running their

'The sound of 'metal

'Exploring openings'

sticks along the fence the sound is linked to kinaesthetics. The adults here support their involvement with noise through offering metal objects to hang on strings alongside the hut. The resonance and vibration within metal gives a very distinctive sound.

Creative outdoor areas should have a variety of experiences that explore the sound, reflection and use of metal.

'Man-made experiences'

Children are orally stimulated before birth. Some expectant mothers wear a metal pendant with an inner ball that creates a chime of a particular pitch. When this noise is heard after the baby is born it has a soothing effect since it is associated with the security of being in the womb. The sounds that surround children should be a balance of stimulation and harmony. Young babies take so much from the environment that as adults we have filtered out that it is very easy to bombard them with too much stimulation rather than allowing them to root themselves to someone.

Metal can be used for gentle outdoor chimes played by the wind for babies; toddlers can enjoy chime spaces that are full of metal tubes to run through

'Loud junk music'

'Delicate sounds'

and dance within. One aspect of any instrument is that there is enough space for the sound vibration. Creating sound walls with metal tubes, pan lids, metal car wheel hubcaps – will all need to be suspended a short distance away from the wall to create effective sound.

Imagine the joy of creating a musical tree covered with stainless steel rings that hum when you stand near to them – use a stainless steel musical wand to play the rings and there will be potential of wondrous musical opportunities.

Young children are kinesthetic and when movement is at the core of the outdoor area, we can use children's feet and movement as music. Offer Wellingtons, shoes or clogs with metal tips and watch to see the change in movement as the children enjoy auditory stimulation linked to kinetics – children start to dance on drain covers, even tap their feet whilst they are standing.

'Food for the hedgehog'

Metal spoons and metal pans make the best mud pies but since they are constantly damp it is worth considering the type of metal you use as many will rust very quickly. I would say however that rust is however a part of a cycle of decay and can be used as an opportunity for discussion of environmental issues.   Real pots and pans supported role play to create pretend food inside, this was applied to play outside through the creation of food for a hedgehog. The containers that were provided included colanders, measures tubes and bowls to provide choice and exploration.

Children under three engage in transformational play through most of their day since their pliable brain is creating connections between experiences. This enables them to store frameworks of understanding until they make a new discovery. The provision of metal materials inside and out will enable children to extend their thinking and application of their ideas.

Introduce hollow stainless steel balls to the plastic guttering and the visual stimulation stimulates toddlers to engage in transporting and trajectory schemas for long blocks of time - not seen with wooden or plastic balls.

The learning story detailed here shows how a young group of children used simple stainless steel materials to explore a series of experiences full of curiosity and intrigue. The metal balls are visually very attractive and enticed the first child to explore a reflection of her face, this lead to a connection between two 2 year olds as they compared faces and objects reflected in the gold and green balls.

The focus changed to transporting the balls, they found a soft liner and used it to move the balls around the area. The range of weights and types of ball offered them a challenge as they moved around the flexible basket. Phrases such as 'too heavy on my hands', 'Its going,

nooo! falling out', ' Take this away', 'That good eh?' The children took the balls out of the basket and rolled them down slopes and up banks. One little girl took the basket and changed it into a hat. Peepo games ensued for five minutes and then the balls were 're-discovered' near the guttering area. The trellis barrier gives a wonderful surface for posting objects through, weaving and supporting tubing and guttering.   The use of a basket at the beginning of the guttering chute gives children a focal, visual point to get the balls down the tube. The children put the metal balls down the tubes and ran with delight to the other side or peeped through the holes to see if they had come through.

There are three fixed ridged tubes in the area that were used briefly by the very youngest children as a first exploration. The two and a half year old group used them to roll the balls back up the slope and out onto the grass area near the towers.

To extend the interest a metal framework of towers were provided to allow more manipulation and alteration of the slope and gradient. A basket of mixed balls were offered and again the metal shiny balls and a solid heavy wooden ball were selected over plastic. Two children engaged at first building up and laying out a long pathway of guttering and then ran down the length of it trying to race the ball.

The same children used the next level of challenge on the woodland site, where some of the older children had created a series of bamboo chutes suspended from a tree. The chute is supported by ropes and can be finely balanced to make balls stop or pivot a tube to go down a layer. The metal balls were selected again, even though they rotate and stick at the bamboo joints. The chute starts above head height which added to their excitement because the movement could be heard before seen.

The little boy rolled one metal ball down the chute, helping it along with his hands. The ball stopped when it bumped into another ball at the bottom of the run. He now picked up both balls, ran to the top

of the run and placed both balls onto it together – he smiled as he watched them both race down the chute together. He

repeated this a few times using both balls, either letting one go first and then the other or letting them both go at the same time. The bamboo chutes offer a challenge to the two year olds due to their height, their inconsistent diameter and their naturally uneven inner surface.

The fascination with metal balls was taken further through the water fountain at the centre.   It was purchased in response to the children's interest in circularity and metal. The three stainless steel globes enable more comparison of the distortion of reflections, fascination with the technology of the machine ' we have to put more in before it will start' generated a wide range of activity around the area with watering cans and buckets. When the pump started the children used their hands to roll across the surface, comments were made about the range of temperature from 'My fingers so cold' to ' feel it getting warmer, hold the ball it getting warm!'. They made patterns in the water on the surface and talked of ' sprinkles and wobbles in the water' and of course the discovery of water pressure to squirt at each other.

The focus on metals and spheres is of continuing interest to the

children. They found stainless steel rings and created wire shapes to create the entranceway between two trees to the Woodland site. The circles and rings have been suspended on rope so that they can turn and rotate in the wind, each day the children turn and handle them as they step between the trees and into the woodland. The metal rings had lead into twisting and bending willow and dogwood into shapes to hang.

Metal is one of the elements of the earth and should therefore be an integral opportunity and experience of the 0-3 play area.

'Metal' resources

Provide galvanised metal buckets
Stainless steel rings
Metal jugs
Stainless steel balls
Metal instruments such as tubular bells,
singing wands, giant sleigh bells
Metal spoons, stainless steel mixing bowls of varying sizes
Wire soft enough to manipulate
Metal trays
Measuring spoons
Metal spoons linked together
Wire baskets
Seives
Colanders
Potato mashers
Shaky eggs
Cutlery sorting tray
Dishwasher metal basket
Tin foil
Recycled catering trays
Metal water fountain
Wind turbine
Wind spiral
Carabinas
Metal gardening tools
Chains of different lengths and various sizes

Fire, Light and Shadow

When fire is mentioned in connection to young children many adults voice words such as risk. However, if we look at the wider view and see fire as warmth then young children can experience the cosiness of snuggling in a blanket, or sitting in a warm sleeping bag to have a story. Warmth, and ultimately the creation of fire, is a core part of the nature kindergartens and schools in the Scandinavian countries. The searching for wood, the method of collecting, gathering of the kindling, the way the wood is transported are all powerful schemas that motivate people into adult hood. The sorting of wood into different diameters and lengths, the laying of the wood to create a good base are all about mathematical and scientific concepts. The feeling of success after the creation of a spark from scratch, the self accomplishment that people feel when they have made a fire that will ultimately cook their food and keep them warm is all at the core of the current Forest School work that is firmly established in the Baltic countries and is now taking hold across the United Kingdom.

Family units in parts of the world have a closer connection to the elements than others. The culture that a child grows up in both the wider elements of the country and the closer community influence the experiences that children are exposed to. For many families they are not in a place that readily connects them to Nature and therefore the ease of turning on a switch is so easy that there is no drive to explore different ways of keeping warm or getting light. The element of fire in these communities has become one of a cooker, central heating or a gas fire, which are far harder for a child to interpret as being hot. Without flames there are few visual cues to heat. Some families seek out a re-connection to the elements through a park, a holiday to the mountains, a remote valley, but many live their lives totally in a manufactured, commercial world with high levels of sophistication that has edged out nature. If our society is going to save the planet we need first to understand it in all its' forms.

'Patterns of fire in New Zealand'

If we look at examples from around the world there are huge variations in the contact children have with fire.
The photograph is taken in a place near the Norwegian border where the community has created a large fire bowl for use by everyone, with warming shelters near by, so that young children can be part of the group gathered around the pit to get warm and

'The warming hut'

ultimately get hot food. The temperature of –30 degrees C in a remote space necessitates the use of fire. Children in many rural areas use fire as the means of cooking. The small group of children in our observations have had varying experiences of fire. By the age of two all were aware of the heat coming from flames and were also fascinated by them. The candles on a birthday cake are testament to that!

For a child under three there are elements of this that create the same feelings. Being outside and wrapped up warm and cosy is a root feeling of security, being part of a group that is working together and linking in to that

'Pretend fire with real food'

'Pretend fire'

process gives a sense of community. That process does not always lead to lighting a fire, often the attraction of den building is of protection and warmth, children collect and gather sticks and put them into a pile to represent fire. The two and three year

olds mimic the risks of the fire, warming hands and cooking on pretend stoves, using words such as 'hot, hot, hot', 'burney', ouch!! These play experiences are a rehearsal for life and such are very valuable, children can be their own assessors of risk if we allow them to experience things with us nearby. Fire obviously has to be monitored, to safeguard children when they are

'Hiding in shadows'

learning about what it represents. When we work with fire we have clear expectations of what the adults will do and what children can do themselves. For a young child there are obviously going to be close connections with the adults, the important aspect to hold onto is how fundamental the human need is for social gathering, sitting in a circle that traditional came from fireside experiences is in our human psychy, and can be seen from aboriginal groups in Australia, to meeting huts in the Congo, to circle time in Scotland.

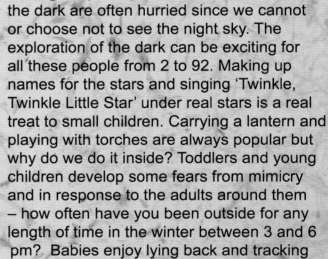

If we view fire as light – the possibilities are much broader, natural dappled shade under trees, areas of clear light and shade create different atmospheres that very young babies enjoy. We can create perspex patterns of colour

Many children do not experience true darkness anymore due to the light pollution from streetlights. Lifestyles have become linked closely to cars rather than walking, so pick up from school or care in the dark are often hurried since we cannot or choose not to see the night sky. The exploration of the dark can be exciting for all these people from 2 to 92. Making up names for the stars and singing 'Twinkle, Twinkle Little Star' under real stars is a real treat to small children. Carrying a lantern and playing with torches are always popular but why do we do it inside? Toddlers and young children develop some fears from mimicry and in response to the adults around them – how often have you been outside for any length of time in the winter between 3 and 6 pm? Babies enjoy lying back and tracking

'To the unaware they are just tubes'

a torch light beam across the ceiling, or lying underneath a pram canopy arch with uv resistant semi transparent fabrics draped over it and watching the movement of leaves in the soft sunshine. There is light shadow and pattern in all types of spaces that adults do not see. The fixed tubes were used with balls. When one ball failed to re-appear, several children spent some time looking up the tubes, closing over vents to make patterns.

'The light show looking up the tube'

The children have candles at the snack table and this little boy was enthralled by the disappearance of the flame and the movement of the smoke. He was aware of the risk and looked at the adult to say "it's hot, now it's gone". The adult relit the candle and the boy was transfixed. He watched two candles for a block of time and then chose to blow them out. "Look I make smoke, it going up - why is it going up" The adult relit the candle many times to talk about the way the smoke moved and how the candle flickered and moved. At no point did he attempt to touch the candle because he knows the reality and consequences. The following sessions offered a candle sorting session, lighting

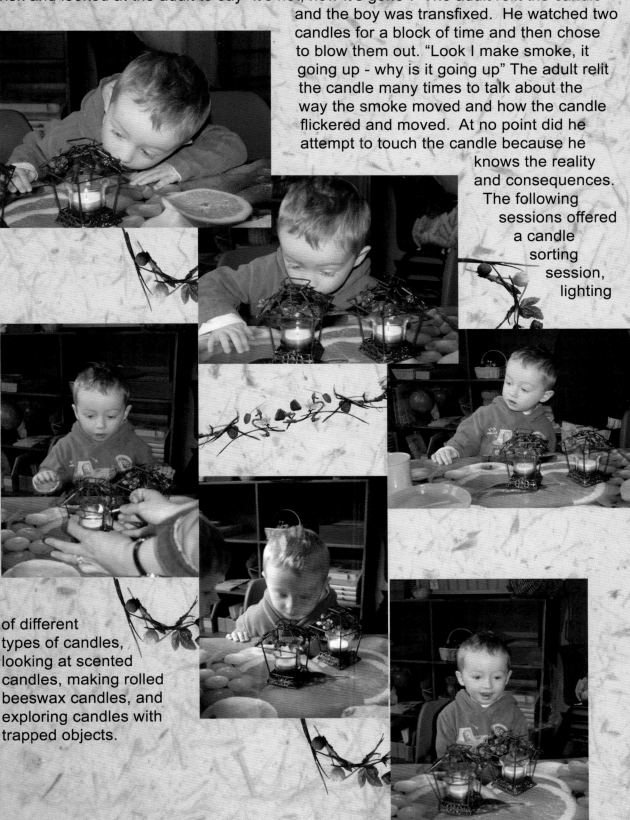

of different types of candles, looking at scented candles, making rolled beeswax candles, and exploring candles with trapped objects.

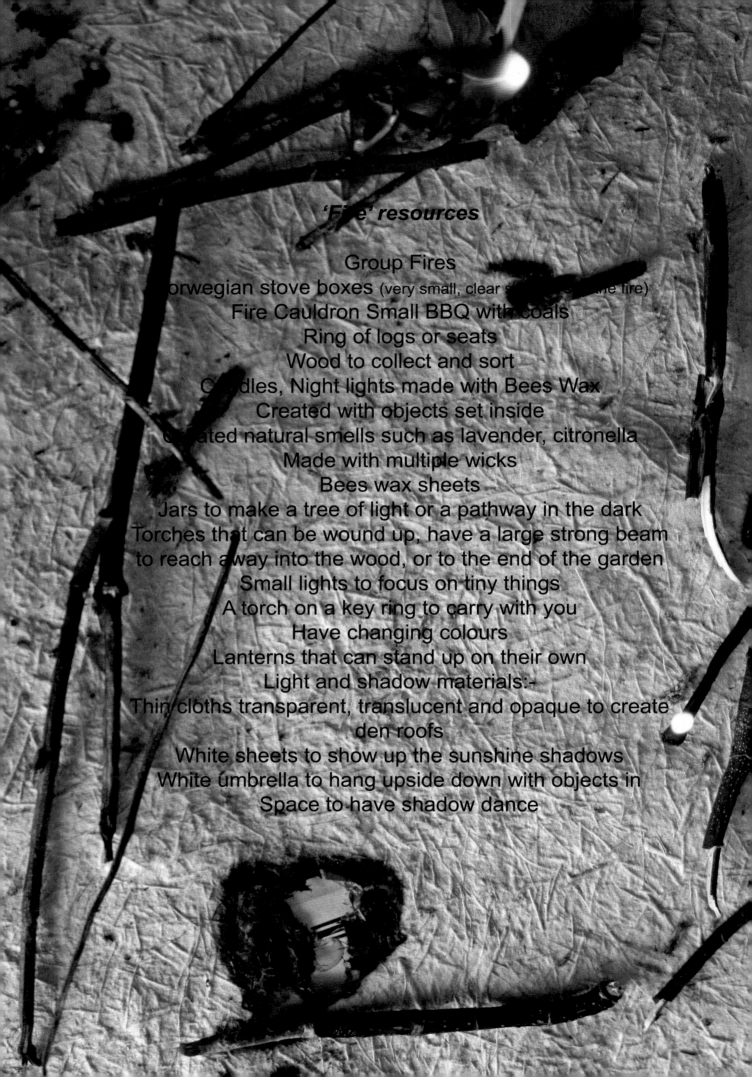

'Fire' resources

Group Fires
Norwegian stove boxes (very small, clear s___ ___ ___ fire)
Fire Cauldron Small BBQ with coals
Ring of logs or seats
Wood to collect and sort
Candles, Night lights made with Bees Wax
Created with objects set inside
Created natural smells such as lavender, citronella
Made with multiple wicks
Bees wax sheets
Jars to make a tree of light or a pathway in the dark
Torches that can be wound up, have a large strong beam
to reach away into the wood, or to the end of the garden
Small lights to focus on tiny things
A torch on a key ring to carry with you
Have changing colours
Lanterns that can stand up on their own
Light and shadow materials:-
Thin cloths transparent, translucent and opaque to create
den roofs
White sheets to show up the sunshine shadows
White umbrella to hang upside down with objects in
Space to have shadow dance

Animals

Imagine a world where the lines were harsh and unyielding, the textures were consistent and variation is unheard of. Does it inspire you? Now imagine a place where the carpet changes every day, the ceiling is a myriad of different colours, light, shadow and movement. The feelings and movement completely surround you, sometimes breezy, sometimes cold, other warm. Unexpected wonders fly by, sometimes full of colour and sometimes full of noise and movement. If we really want children to thrive we need to let their connection to nature nurture them. Other living things especially animals fascinate children with their movement, appearance and behaviour. Investigation and observation are often at odds with a very young childs ability to control their body movements. We need to protect wildlife but also understand that children may not be as morally upstanding or aware at the age of two.

The landscape that young children are exposed to has a direct link to the type and quality of experience they encounter on a daily basis. Every early years centre should have an outdoor space for all the children in its care. The access to fresh air is a vital part of growing that can be through going out of the centre for a walk in a nearby park, having rest time in 'outdoor rooms', or playing in areas that are connected to the centre for long blocks of time.

Outdoor spaces in the United Kingdom have very few real dangers in terms of mini-beasts, such as poisonous spiders that you might find in Austrailia or bears in the Yukon in Canada. Yet some centres still have a tangible concern about taking babies and toddlers into outside spaces because of the animal life.

'Feeling mini-beasts'

Children always have a fascination and joy at seeing an animal or an insect arrive unexpectedly. Imagine the joy you might feel watching thousands of butterflies take off and then hold that emotion and transfer it to the way that a child feels when they see one butterfly. The animal kingdom is full of amazing things and mind blowing ingenuity and skill, children see this aspect of nature in fact some would say that they are part of it and so have an intrinsic understanding of what lies at the core of it. Some adults have lost that link or connectedness to animals whether the animal is a common tiny bug or the majestic largest whale swimming the oceans.

There are moments when the investigation goes a step too far with children, where a gentle desire to touch a beetle leads to something more serious. The sequence of photographs were taken when one little girl of 2 yrs old was playing on the slide. When she came towards it at the beginning of the session she noticed that a small beetle was trying to make it's way up the slide. After several seconds of watching it, the little girl started to mimic the behaviour at the end of

the slide by holding on to the side of the slide and moving her legs up and down. The beetle was still not moving very far due to the angle of the slide. The little girl cupped her hands as if to help the beetle up, as the beetle touched her hands she pulled back for a few seconds and then moved forward again. This time she kept her hands beside the beetle as it used her fingers as a prop to get up the slide. At about half way up the slide the little girl let go of the beetle and said "WEEEEE" as it slid to the bottom. Now this could be

interpreted as cruel but the little girl did not do it for that reason, I am sure that she was transferring her joy of getting up the slide and down again onto an emotion for the beetle. Peripheral planting of other plants and shrubs that attract insects such as buddleia will ensure that there is a lot of visual movement in the area. There are a number of species of this shrub to give a range of colours and it should be cut back each year to maintain healthy growth.

We can encourage wildlife into our spaces through simple wood piles, quieter areas with less 'traffic'. Ken Jaffey (USA) suggests that we use clear tunnels through small slopes so that we expose the world of worms to mobile babies and toddlers.

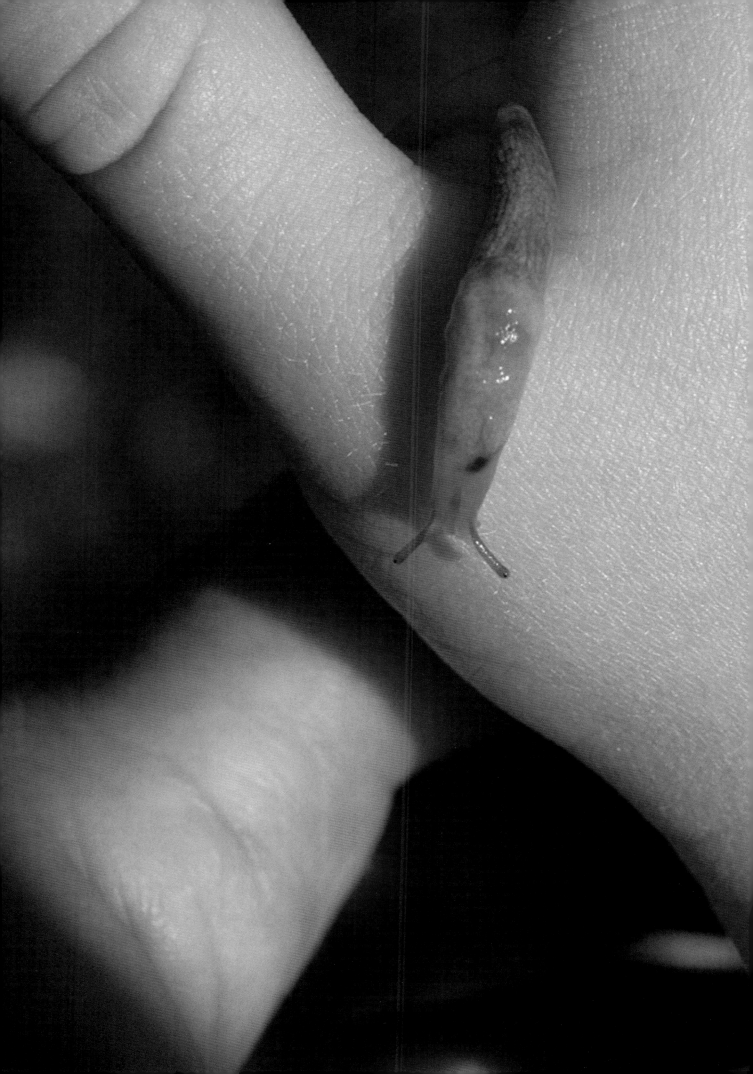

A little girl found an earthworm while digging in the woods. She held it up to show her friend and he wanted a worm too, "I show you, you got a spade? Dig here, not there, here lots" They both dug in the moist soil together. She found a large one and offered it to her friend. Without discussing it he gave her the small worms he found while she gave him her large worms. "I got a baby one, a tiny baby one" "Mine is the daddy one and that is the mummy one, lots of mummy ones". He put all but one of his worms onto a leaf and then gently cuddled his special worm. Staff extended the experience by offering the children a selection of magnifying glasses to enable them to look closely at earthworms and other bugs. The children went into the Kindergarten garden and looked for worms and other mini beasts. They learnt that there were bugs

such as slugs that made holes in their plants while earthworms hid under the ground and made tunnels. The Kindergarten staff created a mini wormery between two sheets of Perspex to allow children to see the tunnels made by earthworms and purchased a large outdoor wormery used to recycle greenwaste produced from snacktime.
A few days later a child picked

up a rock and discovered a nest of Millipedes curled up at the base of a tree. The children named them as worms and brought one to the adult in the area. He brought their attention to the many legs and they compared it to a worm from the wormery. Some of the group were very keen to hold the millipede but due to fine motor control the adult suggested they allow the millipede to choose where it wanted to go. The millipede's were taken very carefully for a short holiday in the nursery building to support some of the more fearful children and encourage them to touch the millipede's in a more familiar and secure environment.

Bird tables are often used in centres, do consider the view a young child has and how they can access it. Either create steps up to the window so that children can see out at the right level, or create a low level feeding zone perhaps at the end of a tunnel to focus attention on one area.

'Consider the height'

This little two year old girl found a bird hide made by older children. She used her binoculars and tried hard to spot the birds she could hear all

around her, but all she saw was the greenery. She looked down; spotted a handy root, climbed onto it and now she could see over the wall of the bird hide and see the birds. The bird hide is a permanent feature of the woodland site but is often used as a cosy spot to chat.

'Problem solving to find a handy root to stand on'

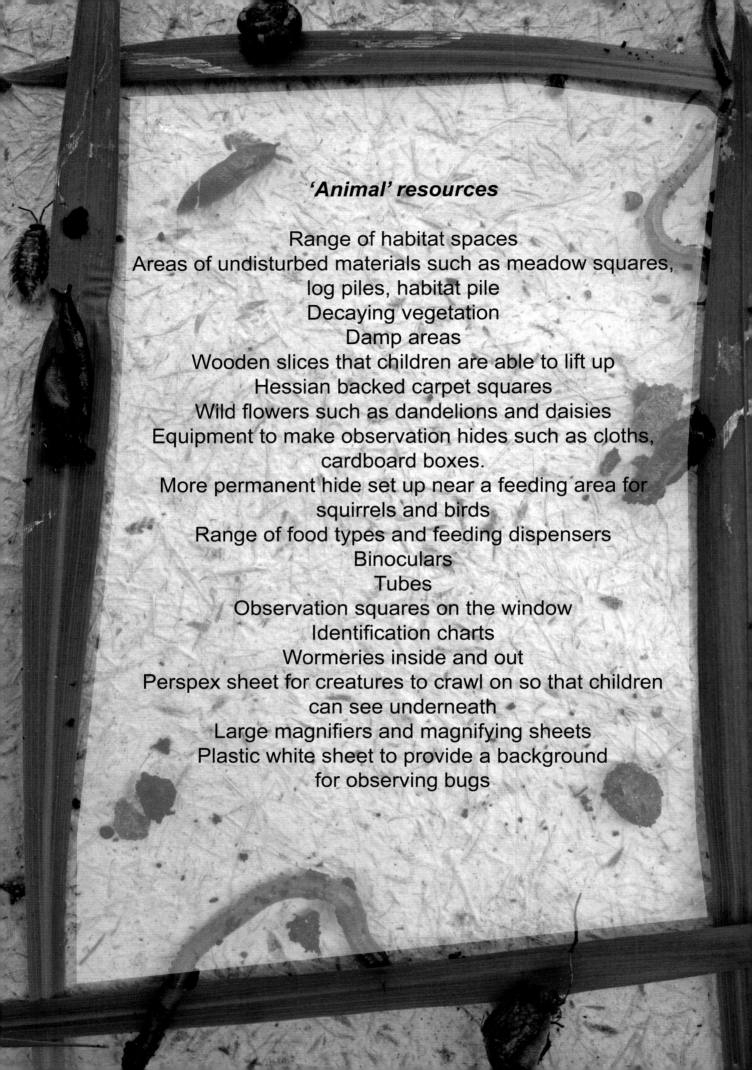

'Animal' resources

Range of habitat spaces
Areas of undisturbed materials such as meadow squares,
log piles, habitat pile
Decaying vegetation
Damp areas
Wooden slices that children are able to lift up
Hessian backed carpet squares
Wild flowers such as dandelions and daisies
Equipment to make observation hides such as cloths,
cardboard boxes.
More permanent hide set up near a feeding area for
squirrels and birds
Range of food types and feeding dispensers
Binoculars
Tubes
Observation squares on the window
Identification charts
Wormeries inside and out
Perspex sheet for creatures to crawl on so that children
can see underneath
Large magnifiers and magnifying sheets
Plastic white sheet to provide a background
for observing bugs

Children are fascinated by plants that are all around them. If we imagine the feeling of awe and inspiration that would come over us if we were moving through a bamboo walkway, or a forest of redwoods towering above us, we can begin to understand the perception that children have when they are in a forest or walking through a summer garden packed full of colours, smells and textures. To someone who is less that a metre tall the smallest tunnels of willow will seem as if they were a forest, a log to scramble over feels like a mountain, the size of a new conker in your hand feels enormous. The spaces that we offer need vegetation in them, not artificial grass and flowers that have little sensory exploration.

Every aspect of a plant offers a learning opportunity to all children, but especially to the youngest children in our care. The first time you see a root, a leaf, a flower, a fruit or in fact explore plants closely, it takes your breath away. I have residual memories of trying to unfurl a fern leaf just as it was emerging and attempting to wrap it up again, because someone had told me

that the elves in the wood had to do it every night to protect the leaf. As a young child I 'could' believe in fairy dresses made from rose petals and spun spider silk. The world I lived in, obviously created for me and guided by my family was a place where plants and nature had a variety of functions. There was gardening in order to harvest, cook and eat but also to imaginative times where leaves were held together with pine needles to make magic carpets. Working with plants can provide us with food, colour, warmth, sound and much, much more. The work we do at the nature kindergarten is designed to reconnect children to nature. The children, from two years old, are part of the process of planting, tending and harvesting their food. The vegetables, fruit from miniature trees or vegetation coppiced from pots are used to make everything from jam to potato soup, from plant dyes to sustainable materials for creativity. The area is not large but the children know that crisps come from potatoes, that lavender is blue when it grows, and that the favourite food for slugs are new shoots in their own potager. Centres can create wonderful spaces very quickly with tyres. The centre featured in these photos changed a tarmac zone into a wonderful space for children under three.

Changing Spaces

While digging in a forest site the 2 and a half year old boy uncovered an orange coloured root. "I found a carrot" he called excitedly and started digging. A four year old boy looked into the hole "That's not a carrot, that is a root" he stated and walked away. The younger child did not respond but continued to dig, uncovering more of the orange root. "Look my carrot is big, I pull it" He tried digging and pulling out the root but could not dislodge it. After about 15 minutes he found a worm and moved away as he had lost interest in uncovering the rest of the root. He made no more comments about 'his carrot'. The awareness that carrots are orange and grow underground was extended in the nursery garden through the provision of a clear Perspex box to show the root growth of both yellow and orange carrots that are grown from seed. Inside the Kindergarten the children explored a basket of vegetables and sorted them according to vegetables growing under the ground and those growing above ground.

This sensorial nursery garden for children aged birth to five years was developed out of an area of tarmac within a walled space. A corner of the garden had the tarmac removed.

Willow arches, a cosy seating area for toddlers, plants designed to stimulate all the senses and

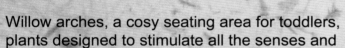

stepping stones were placed in this area. Another area was filled with sand and a rowing boat was added for older children to climb into and younger ones to pull themselves up against. Tractor tyres were filled and used for a variety of purposes - a herb garden, a grassy turf area, soil and a plant space to use for small world play. The tyres were arranged on the tarmac to create pathways. Posts were erected to allow a shade cloth to be used on sunny days.

Exploring Fruit

Horse chestnuts were brought in by a member of the team to develop a schema on developing and enclosing. Opening a fruit pod still holds a sense of awe for many people. The fresh new skin of the conker shines within the soft white flesh of the seed case. The discovery of the fruit held a great fascination because they had a dull spiky exterior.

'Exploring the outer surfaces'

'Beginning to explore openings - the moment when the seed is revealed for the first time'

'The challenge of putting it back in'

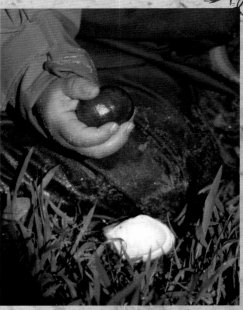

'The enjoyment of the conker, its shiny appearance and the smoothness of the seed itself'

Grass

Grass is such a simple word for something that represents a myriad of species. The variety of grass on our planet is truly astounding. To a child under three they offer a wonderful resource to:

- Lie in
- Lie on
- Roll over
- Crawl through
- Hide behind
- Touch and feel
- Weave
- Move
- Explore
- Pick
- Stroke
- Eat

'Touching and feeling'

'Waving and moving'

'Looking through'

Grass can survive anywhere so it a very flexible resource for early years environments. There are and increasing number of children with allergies so this should be considered when the pollen starts to develop.

'Having a large scale experience'

Flowers

Flowers offer us colour, scent and a range of textures and pattern. Each year sees the cycle of nature emerge, enabling children and adults to find, touch and experience it for the first time. The apparently simple process of reaching out to touch a flower actually involves a high level of thinking and problem solving for very young children. The sensorial stimulation of flowers provides motivation for movement, the curiosity and investigation drive children's learning forward.

First with the finger reaching out   then with the hand...

Taking confidence to reach to another place

Picking with third finger and thumb

Picking with first finger and thumb

Holding on with just enough pressure

Seeds

As every gardener will tell you, seeds are the hope for the future. Nature offers such a range that children and adults can explore them for years and never know them all. A child found a dandelion and since it had no defined structure or resistance the child's finger move over and through the seed head. Seeds started to fall off, at which point she used a newly developed skill to close first finger and thumb to pull them off. She stood and watched as they floated away across the grass.

The wind takes them from the child's fingers.

She dances after the seeds and finds a couple of clumps waiting for her nearby. The seeds stick to her fingers.

She goes back to the stem and encloses the head of the dandelion in her palm so that the calyx is enclosed.

After holding the dandelion for a few moments, she starts to stroke the head gently.

Lays it down and then dances away.

Leaves and Wood

Trees have a very special place in our lives. I am not prone to evangelical statements but I do believe that when we are surrounded by something that dwarves us by the years it has seen, its endurance and strength it does seem to have a calming effect. Perhaps it is about putting human beings into a bigger picture, moving beyond the

individuality. An aim would be to have a tree in every school and centre in the country so that children can lie under its leaves and babies can gaze up through branches as they fall asleep. It is possible with a creative brain and a vision to make under three outdoor spaces, natural and long lasting to put something back into the environment.

Collecting and gathering is a schema that is repeated throughout life. When we talk it becomes apparent that children make petal perfume through the process of collecting and gathering bits to make the perfume, parents tell me that they made mud soup, collecting and gathering, grandparents tell me of pretend fires they made, collecting and gathering bits and pieces. Many people seem to think that children have lost their creativity, I feel that they have not,

however it may be a little lost and often masked by commercial experiences. Our role is to create opportunities to connect to nature.

A group of children were 'wandering' and after an adult suggestion started to make mud pies and when the adult realised that they had no experience she started to role play the situation, asking for green water, a perfect stick to mimic stirring and making soup. After a few minutes the children joined her, making their own pots of soup and pretending to make a fire. The children who were younger engaged at a level that was about filling and emptying buckets with water, transporting wood and gathering mud.

Children can be very focused on detail rather than the larger picture that adults tend to see. Each stick offers something new, whether it is a nodule, a pattern or a texture. One of the most wonderful experiences I have had, was when a little boy of two years old offered to play with me. At a point in the play he disappeared and came back a little later with his hands held together. He offered them to me and said "lets do it, fix it". In his hand were many bits of one stick. He went on to fix each bit back on and then he asked me to wrap the masking tape around. He had created his own jigsaw based on his favourite stick. Some children have a deeper connection to an element or a place. Whether the memory is lodged from birth or whether

the emotion is linked to a resource such as a stone or water or perhaps a dominant sense. The little boy in the photograph chooses to 'root' himself in the kindergarten through playing a roughly made xylophone in the sound area.

The exploration of the sound of wood can be seen repeatedly across the time he is engaged in play. The woodland site has been designed to both support and extend the experience in the nursery. The little boy played another xylophone that had been made from wood nearby, he explored logs and living trees to hear their sound.

The learning story above shows that these traits and behaviours are within our make-up. Children perceive what is important to adults and respond to it. If we celebrate plastic then it is seen as important. Through providing materials such as wooden discs, small driftwood, angular off cuts and giant shavings we can offer the material for children to collect, gather and transport around the indoor and outdoor rooms.

The child featured in the following story was in an old willow arbour in a garden space. She was motivated by holes. Inside the centre her exploration included poking objects through gaps, engaging with colanders, place mats and a hole in the nose of a teddy!

When she sat in the arbour, her reaction was to explore the texture of the wood, picking up and casting away.

She found a 'stick' that was 'alive and attached'. The experience developed into a contest of strength.

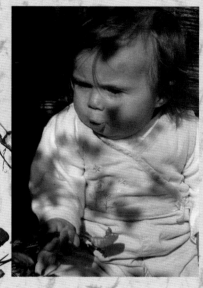

When she fell back she found it all very funny and spent several seconds mimicking the fall.

When the laughs died away she went back to the purpose of poking sticks through the willow.

Children are motivated by the natural world around them. Nature provides an anchor that can give children the awareness of being part of a bigger world. Trees can have that effect on all human beings.

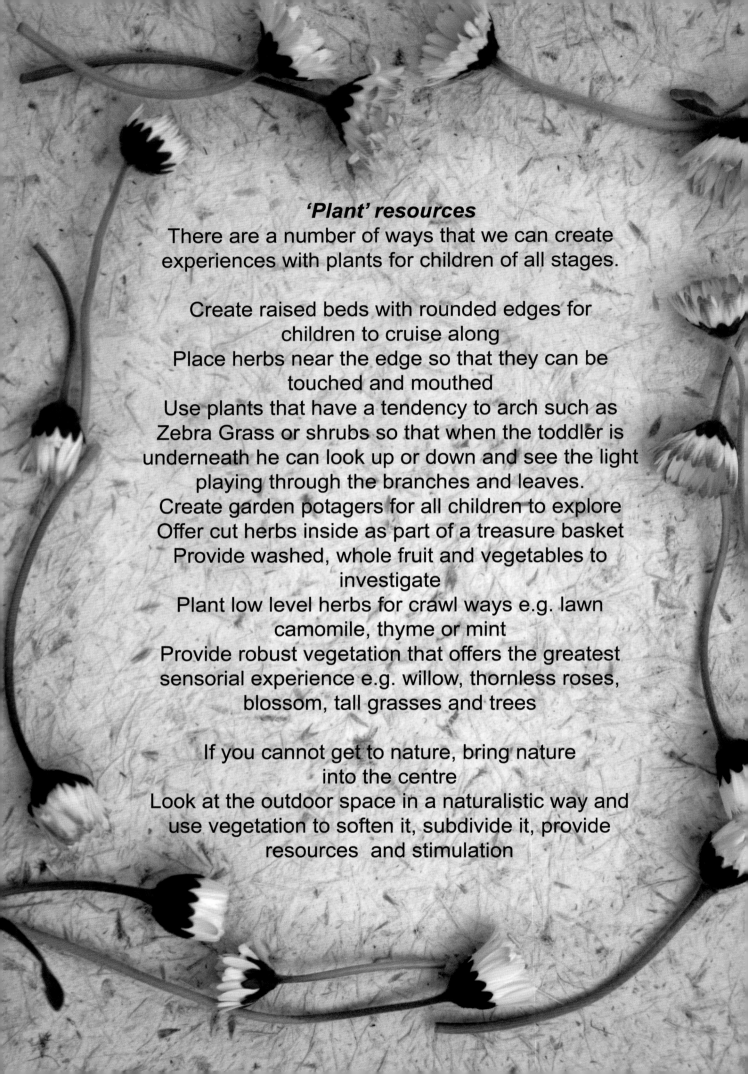

'Plant' resources

There are a number of ways that we can create experiences with plants for children of all stages.

Create raised beds with rounded edges for children to cruise along

Place herbs near the edge so that they can be touched and mouthed

Use plants that have a tendency to arch such as Zebra Grass or shrubs so that when the toddler is underneath he can look up or down and see the light playing through the branches and leaves.

Create garden potagers for all children to explore

Offer cut herbs inside as part of a treasure basket

Provide washed, whole fruit and vegetables to investigate

Plant low level herbs for crawl ways e.g. lawn camomile, thyme or mint

Provide robust vegetation that offers the greatest sensorial experience e.g. willow, thornless roses, blossom, tall grasses and trees

If you cannot get to nature, bring nature into the centre

Look at the outdoor space in a naturalistic way and use vegetation to soften it, subdivide it, provide resources and stimulation

The air we breathe on the planet varies in terms of its quality. Some inner city nurseries are now providing pollution masks as part of their outdoor play. Human beings need good air and very young children are even more susceptible to the impurities that exist through pollution. The book Toxic Childhood has brought many issues to the forefront and it has been positive in initiating discussions about environmental awareness. Organisations such as Eco Schools have enabled hundreds of centres and schools around the world to make a difference to the world in which we live. However, as the smallest members of our society, babies are often disregarded and the materials and substances that exist in their world can be harmful to their long-term development.

All human beings need fresh air and children should be allowed to be out in it as much as possible. The overheated, over processed air that many very young children breath cannot be healthy. The attitude that by being inside protects is actually far from the truth when you compare the number and type of dust mites, allergens and germs.

Walking with prams and units with multiple babies allows some exposure to fresh air. However, it does not enable the mobile children to actually connect to the natural world. Many prams are covered and over padded so that toddlers do not feel the wind or rain on their faces. The communication between the children in the pram and the adult is affected by the way that the seats are positioned. How can a person pushing 5 children in a column push chair respond to what the child sees at the front? Young children need you to stop the pram, crouch beside them and talk to them about what they can see and how they are responding. Babies need the people around them to add a voice to what they see.

The way that we carry very young children varies so much across the world. Babies need to be connected to someone, to create an attachment so that they can hear

or be aware of a heartbeat. If children spend a great deal of time in prams they are actually removed from that security and often have a view of the world that is shown in the photograph.

As soon as children are aware of mobility, I would suggest that it becomes their personal focus. Children should be able to get where they wish and strive for what they want, rather than always being propped up before their bodies are ready to do so. Going outside is part of the world they can explore. Consider how the children in your care get outside. Do you announce that toddlers can go out and open a door holding as many hands as you can or can they crawl out when they wish? Are they able to open a child door to make the transition to go out? Is there any reason why we cannot create a giant cat flap with an arch that is big enough for the toddlers to crawl through? The adult can slide in a sheet to control access, but it would still support the approach of many nurseries in parts of

the world such as Iceland believe "If the children can get there, then it is their time. They should not have to wait for us. The children show us when they are ready, we do not tell them". E.E.C.E.R.A. (2006)

Part of our access to air is the time when we are asleep. Babies and toddlers are rooted in nature and should be allowed to sleep in a cozy sleeping bag in a quiet space outside. Where we have concerns about insects then there are a number of

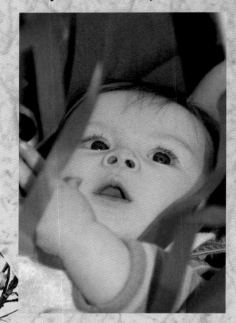

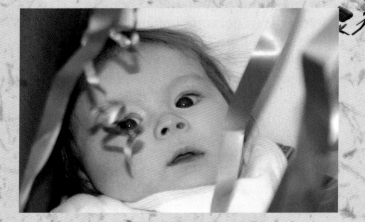

options. Prams have insect nets. In our nature kindergarten we use small hammocks and outdoor mini beds which can be sealed with insects panels and sun/rain sheets. The mini beds have waterproof bases and inflatable mattresses, and sleeping bags to keep the children warm. They can be used from 6 months to 5 years old and so allow flexible use in centres. Some centres have created 'outdoor rooms' with a canopy and removable sides for sleeping. There are a number of high quality baby sleeping bags on the market that are washable and provide cosy warm places for resting.

Moving air and the power that it has to move objects is as much a miracle to adults as it is to young children. The difference is that for adults we need a major impact such as a hurricane, for children under three it is a leaf twirling and birling around in an air pocket. Trees and vegetation are our indicators for the wind and it often makes me question how people in highly urbanized environments can be aware of the high breeze or the wind that can pass through and is gone in a short burst of energy or the gentle wisp that blows across a cornfield. Children and their carers are removed from nature into a space where surfaces are unyielding, areas are enclosed and overprotected and where young children do not experience small indicators of natures change. Adults need to be creative in their celebration of the air we breathe and the effect of the wind. Where there are no natural leaves we can offer natural materials such as Hops, or Rose petals so that they

biodegrade when the wind whisks them away. We can offer pots of grasses that rustle and move as the wind passes by.

This learning story takes place in the summer, when there is naturally a greater connection since the layers of protective clothing have been reduced! The girl in the photo was playing near the cruising wall on a decking area. The wind started to blow and she could sense that there was a change. Raising her head, she looked into the

wind as if to ascertain where it was coming from. For several minutes she moved her head into different positions to feel how the wind could move her hair. At this point she started to clap and laugh to show her

enjoyment and engagement in the experience. The wind died away and her response changed, leading her to move on to something else. This enjoyment of wind and the effect it had on her extended over the block of weather that followed. The next part of her story was to go out in rain and sunshine to play with the wind. Balloons were tied to the fence on a strong string about 50 cm long and the wind pulled and pushed them in a game of 'catch the balloon'! The more the wind tugged and changed direction the greater the laughter. When the wind died away towards the end of the afternoon, she started to push and hit the balloons so that they started to move again. Since the more powerful wind had gone she started to use leaves and feathers provided but the interest had moved on.

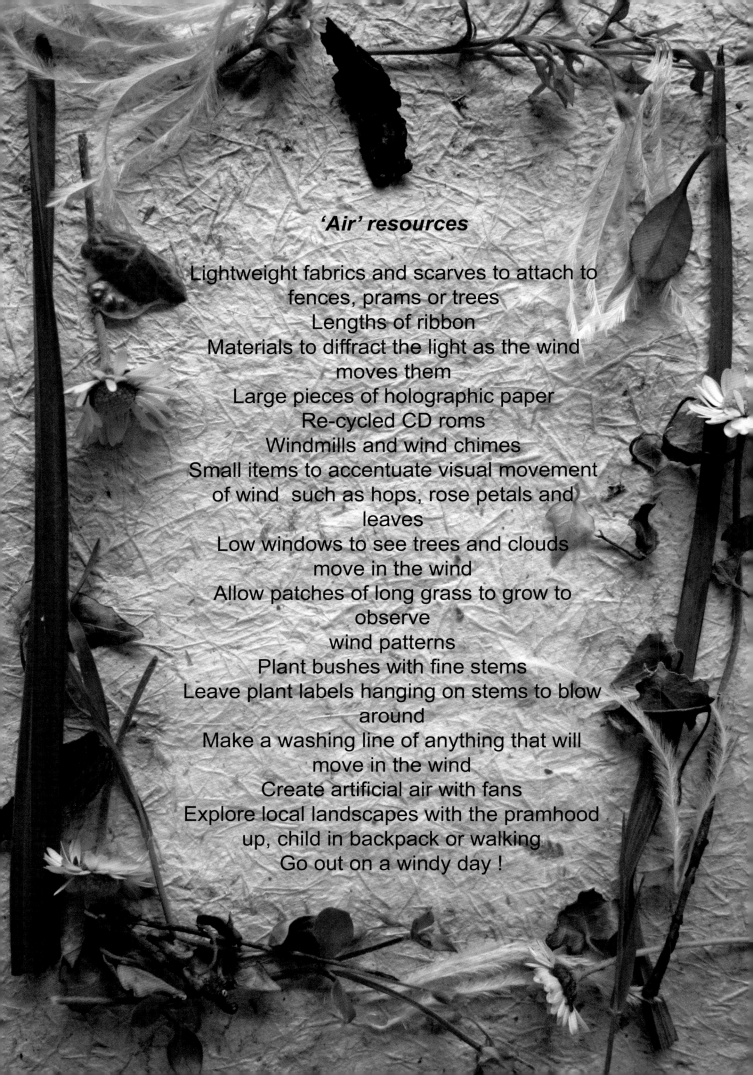

'Air' resources

Lightweight fabrics and scarves to attach to
fences, prams or trees
Lengths of ribbon
Materials to diffract the light as the wind
moves them
Large pieces of holographic paper
Re-cycled CD roms
Windmills and wind chimes
Small items to accentuate visual movement
of wind such as hops, rose petals and
leaves
Low windows to see trees and clouds
move in the wind
Allow patches of long grass to grow to
observe
wind patterns
Plant bushes with fine stems
Leave plant labels hanging on stems to blow
around
Make a washing line of anything that will
move in the wind
Create artificial air with fans
Explore local landscapes with the pramhood
up, child in backpack or walking
Go out on a windy day !

Spaces That We Create

Being three or younger gives you a different perspective on the world and enables the simplest of objects to become something of awe and wonder. These photographs were

taken from the angle of a two year old and show views of an outdoor area that many people never see. Children search out perspectives and views that intrigue and inspire them, often leading to behaviours that some adults find challenging. One view is to consider that we should in fact take these very behaviours of investigation and curiosity and use them in our designs rather than the cocoon that so many very young children are wrapped in. By doing this we can create a place for children to

play that is full of space so that they can create in it through changing open ended resources, holes to peer through, objects to hide behind or a rock to scramble over. The outdoor space

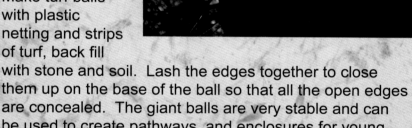

for all children should excite and motivate them.

Make turf balls with plastic netting and strips of turf, back fill with stone and soil. Lash the edges together to close them up on the base of the ball so that all the open edges are concealed. The giant balls are very stable and can be used to create pathways, and enclosures for young children to settle in.

Using the same idea create cruising walls with large tubes of fine landscape netting, back filled with resilient grass seed and compost. The diameter needs to be about 50 cm to give stability and retain moisture. Bend and shape the tubes into 's' bends and barchan shaped areas to give enclosure. Water well to start the germination process. If the area needs more height, plants non poisonous/non-irritant plants such as herbs or cereal crops along the top. Baby curves can be made in the same way to support children who wish to sit against it or sit astride it.

Wooden troughs that are very stable can be planted with objects, with the knowledge that they will be used to 'pull up' so troughs in these areas need to be bolted down to make them stable.

Plants can be used to define crawl ways with low arches of soft vegetation to crawl through. Use soft eco-block and under plant with lawn camomile, dwarf thyme, and ground dwelling marjoram. Create crawl tunnels with strong nylon mesh, plant alongside the tunnel with an edible climber that can be woven into the mesh such as pea plants or nasturtiums. Create them against windows so that the children can be half in the tunnel and feel connected to the children outside.

'Moving into the light'

Entrances and boundaries
The change from one space to another is important for toddlers. The transition between spaces is part of their exploration. As landscape designers we can use these spaces as an integral part of the play process.

'Inspirational fences'

Hiding Spaces
Creating a landscape that builds on children's natural curiosity must include objects for them to hide behind and inside

'A place to reflect'

Reflection
Plastic mirrors can be used outside. In our experience it works most effectively if the framework stays outside and the mirrors are changed. We used black mirrors, silver, green, red and yellow with wonderful results. The babies responded to each new colour in a new way, some touching others grasping.

Light and shadow
Create baby tunnels with UV protection fabric

'Areas of light and shadow'

'Watching the trees dance'

Lower trees with outdoor cradles beneath them with insect nets over for sleeping and observation by recumbent children.
Large white sheets supported above children with cellophane/flowers/shapes put on top.
Water that reflects light in rills and shallow pools 1 cm 2cm deep.
Create water fountains with variable flow rates to enable trickles, jets and flows that children can watch, hear and feel.

Texture

We use the resources that we believe touch children at a deeper level, so that they engage with children on an emotional plane in a way that plastic adult designed materials cannot. Nature provides texture through sand, pebbles, small boulders, bark, shells, etc. These can be integrated into landscape design so that children have bays of sand, pebbles, and bark complimented by large scale features such as the hollow tree trunk featured above.

'Getting inside the texture'

Visual movement

When children are still at the point that they are beginning to move their bodies the brain is still engaged in tracking movement. This is visual movement and enables babies to hold their heads up, looking and connecting movement with a response. There are a number of ways that it is possible to develop visual movement in areas for children before they become mobile such as ribbons hanging from a branch. Visual movement is a stimulus for children. A child can become completely absorbed in watching a bird fly or trees bending and flexing. The landscape can be designed to create visual movement through the trickle fountain pictured on the right, strategic planting of tall grasses and shrubs that can move in response to the wind.

'Trickle fountain'

Colour

Nature provides a complete palette of colours, but all of them have a depth that plastic resources cannot recreate. The tones and tints in nature vary from second to second and from plant to plant. Naturalistic landscapes should be soft to the eye so that children can develop visual perception skills.

'A blend of sound and colour'

Sound
Natures' sounds are often overtaken by other environmental noise. Quiet zones allow children to hear footsteps crunching on stones, birds singing, wind in the trees and their own breathing.

Exploration
Children need environments that they can explore. Designs that have 'hanging basket trees' that can be decorated in a variety of ways with baskets of materials to discover provide small scale experiences. Whereas

woodland or wilder spaces naturally have things to find.

Tyres with wooden circular lids that have different materials to play in such as bark, sand and mud.

Areas that are enclosed, so that children settle to play and feel secure to do so.

Areas that are provided as walk or crawl in spaces so that children can explore when they wish.

Physical challenges
Children need to take risks and push their boundaries in environments that are designed to offer a range of challenges and experiences. At the kindergarten children learn to climb from low benches to high, over sculptures and then into the wildwood to climb over real trees and fallen logs.

The Way That Children Use The Environment

Some of the behaviours we see children demonstrate are developmentally appropriate, such as transporting stones, filling and emptying buckets with mud, enclosing and enveloping plastic beetles in large leaves. In fact, rather than preventing and controlling these behaviours, they should become motivational buttons that we can use to plan children's learning (Warden 1999). Our skill as practitioners is to consider to what extent children's behaviours are caused by our provision.

The schemas outlined below are the most common and children may flow in and out of schema over time. Schemas are evident across all the curricula boundaries and are perhaps a more child centred way of planning and responding to children.

Transporting

Here and there:- looking from where you are to over there (variety of tools such as binoculars/lens/diffraction tube), putting up pulley systems to move objects from here to there and back again, bags and containers to carry objects in.

Going through a boundary

Going through:- Pooh sticks, stepping through gaps and holes, walking through a wood.
Going over:- climbing over logs, stepping over streams, bridges.

Going under:- arches, holes in walls. Walking under low branches, under cloths.
Going around a boundary:- walking around a tree, weaving ribbons around a tree or an area. Interest in fences, boundaries, walls.

Circularity
Circles of wood, cross sections.
Going round and round in a space.
Weaving grasses into hoops, rings.
Holes in leaves.
Holes in the ground by worms, rabbit holes, etc.
Poking holes in the mud with a stick.
Peering through holes to see the view.

Rotation/spiralling
Lines of rocks to create spirals
Spiral forms such as rolled up ferns, spirals on a snail shell.
Spirals drawn on hard surface.
Twisted vines e.g. Honeysuckle.
Watching wind spiral up the leaves on a windy day.
Spinning turning around trees

Enclosing and enveloping
Collecting objects into pockets, pouches.
Wrapping stones and wood in leaves.
Making holes and hiding plastic animals in them.
Wrapping themselves in clothes, coats, gloves.
Hiding inside boxes, dens, spaces.
Hiding objects under leaves, inside old logs.

Filling and emptying

Containers of a variety of sizes and shapes that are made by children.

Using man made containers to fill and empty a few yards away.

Access to water, soil, leaves, fire bricks, etc to put into the containers.

Pockets and pouches to carry around.

Connecting

Lining up sticks, long grasses, leaves in rows both vertical and horizontal.

Connecting objects to build dens, shelters.

Making links with rope, card and grass between bikes, boats, cardboard boxes.

Threading daisy chains.

Making circular wreaths from grass.

Using willow to weave, twist and connect.

Holding hands, making rings.

Using a variety of natural objects to push into holes, connecting many objects to one.

'Handling and manipulation of wood'

Schema Based Resources

General provision of small containers with handles, rucksacks, buckets, baskets, handbags, large leaves, pieces of bark, natural bowls. Clothing with pockets e.g. discovery waistcoat.

Solid materials such as stones, pebbles ,gravel, bricks, sections of wood, short lengths of branch, leaves, twigs, rose petals, hops (dried or fresh), ice.
Viscous or semi-solid such as pretend soups and mixtures, grass, mud (various types), sand and water, gloup, snow, wet leaves.
Liquids such as self-help water from barrel, scented water in barrels, sparkly water with glitter, mud suspension, potting compost in water, soups, 'made by children.

Objects to use to fill and empty
Solids; trailor, diggers, boxes, wheelbarrows, sand pulleys and lifts, buckets, empty pots and barrels.
Viscous; flatter bowls and trays, large leaves to attach together, coconut shells, scallop shells, bark hollows in trees, trees roots, dips cut out of logs.
Liquid; tubes, funnels to create siphons, cups, old wheels to create water wheels, objects with a pouring lip, slopes to run the water down, guttering.

Materials to manipulate
Ropes, wire, dogwood, hazel, willow, slices of wood, vegetation, tubing, wicker rings, tyres (variety of sizes).

Conversations about the methodology

Starting conversations about a joint vision for the youngest children in our care is of paramount importance if there is going to be a persistent change in provision.

There are a number of statements that are made to me about babies and toddlers going outside. It is undoubtedly a mind set change for some people, but that should not offer too great a challenge. The process should start with conversations to try to reflect on the values that lie behind the statements. In order to promote this I have summarised my approach to or opinion of a series of issues that often conceptually, prevent outdoor play with very young children. There is no one answer to all the challenges that environments and teams have, use these opinions as a starting point to talk about the views of the staff team.

What do you do if they get wet? The first aspect is to accept is that they will get wet, since a connection to nature is that children want to and need to engage fully with the elements. 'Warm wet' in the summer is less uncomfortable than the 'Cold wet' that colder temperatures or wind chill create.

Where will you change them? In the ideal world every nursery would be designed with large changing areas, outdoor toilets, with storage for waterproofs/clothes at the door. However most centres will need to be creative in how they work through the challenge. The We-Go Wet systems hang over the indoor cloakroom hooks, or outside on a railing. The waterproofs cover the whole child and strap tightly over the Wellington boot so the water does not trickle down the waterproof and into the boot.

How will you minimize the amount of water in the indoor space? Create a visual space for children to go to when they want to take off the wet kit. The We-Go Wet™ has a large purple mat that can be taken off the backdrop and put onto the carpet/ floor. Matting at the door should be highly absorbant and quick drying. Non slip flooring minimizes risk of slippage.

How can you support the children who do not want/enjoy being wet?
There is an emotional strength that lies within some children that enables them to deal with discomfort more easily. This can be exacerbated by adult response. There is a role for the adult to demonstrate the way we cope with discomfort and support children to persevere with a situation through more physical activity or improved clothing. There is a responsibility for the centre to provide appropriate clothing such as waterproof winter suits or waterproof rompers that go over the Wellington boot.

'Minus 22 degrees centigrade !!'

How do you get them all dressed? No play environment could function without a degree of child autonomy. Outdoor play preparation is the same. With very young children it does involve a higher degree of adult support. Some centres do create a greater challenge by wanting to get all the children ready at one point 'to go out'. By using a staggered/free flow access to the outdoor play area, the pressure on the adult decreases and the process becomes a more positive experience for all concerned.

By the age of around 18months children enjoy the challenge of putting some or all of their own clothes on. Although it takes a greater commitment at the start the achievement can really affect how effective the centre is at getting children outside efficiently. Give children their own basket of equipment to put on and then store it beside their peg. Waterproofs are sized in such a way that most children will fit into a general size. Open legged rompers with Velcro straps enable mobile children to take them off over their Wellington boots more easily than elasticated cuffs. However I have seen Wellington boots suspended inside the legs of the toddler waterproofs, held in by the elastic strap. Baby waterproofs tend to have complete coverage with integral booties.

'Laughing in the rain'

Create changing areas near the outdoor area so that children can start to change themselves.

How do you keep them warm? Warmth comes from within so children need to have the fuel such as food or milk to give them energy to keep warm. Movement generates internal warmth and is the solution to children feeling cold. The lack of circulation through narrowing of the capillaries is the cause of cold fingers. The way to increase blood flow is to make the heart pump faster. So create songs and stories that require movement.
Warm fleeces are wonderful but are not windproof so make sure that little ones have a wind barrier over the top. Most of the heat is lost out of the head, so hats with ear flaps can be used for most of the year. Gloves need to be at hand so use a box or cupboard near to the door to get them easily. The 'We-Go Wet'™ has pockets to take hats and gloves so that they can be accessed or abandoned whilst still outside. Use elastic to tie together the gloves and thread it through the arms of the coat to prevent lost gloves. The top tip is to monitor the length of the elastic, otherwise gloves end up in puddles and serving as 'pets' dragging behind!! Waterproof gloves allow children to play in water and snow on colder days.

How do you keep them dry? The same is true as above. The need to dry clothing is the source of a lot of concern in centres due to the number of children. The only solution that we have seen is a drying cupboard. Which is positioned in the entrance way. The cupboards are bought as a unit and plugged in. The gentle heat dries out equipment in less than an hour, which is of key importance for those centres that share waterproofs and clothing needs to be dried to send home.

What do you do if they eat everything? Create a space with plants that they can touch and mouth such as herbs and grass, until they know the difference. There should be lower staff ratios so that they can stay near the children who are continuing to mouth, just as you would inside the centre. There are lists of recommended/poisonous plants available on the website.

What do you do if they fall over? Pick them up and don't overreact, since some children accentuate the emotion to call for attention. If that attention is gained through play or conversation, the stumble is often seen as a minor event.
Safety surfaces are often suggested as a solution. Children will develop the internal mechanism to cope with slope and changing gradients if they are allowed to engage with them. The safety surface can reduce impact injury, but it does not solve all the challenges. It can take away the need for children to become risk aware. Play is all about exploration for all ages of child, the risks children take are part of that exploration. Staff need to have a hip belt with an emergency first aid kit in it, so that they can respond immediately whilst outside.

'Assessing the risk'

What do you do to stop any accidents? The nature of risk assessments is that they show that the team have considered possibilities and done all they can to prevent an accident **before** it occurs. However some hazards noted on risk assessments are also very unlikely to happen so therefore they have a low overall ranking. Teams need to look at those incidents that are highly likely but of a low hazard type such as a tumble.
Care of grounds, adult support when toddlers are unsure, increases in challenge built into the environment, opportunities for children to learn to self assess are all integral to risk assessments. It is this methodology that will ultimately create a 'safer' environment. The place where no accidents will happen does not exist. By their nature risk assessments have to be a blend of living and limitation.

'Balancing freedom with safety'

Bibliography and Useful Reading

Abbott, I. and Moylett, H. (1997) <u>Working with the under threes</u>; Responding to children's needs

Athey.C. (1990) <u>Extending thought in young children: a parent teacher partnership.</u> Paul Chapman Pub

Arbor Day Foundation website - www.arborday.org

Bredecamp, S.(1997) <u>Developmentally Appropriate Practice in Early Childhood Programmes</u> Washington NAEYC

Bruer. J. (1999) <u>The Myth of the first three Years</u>. The Free Press

Christie R and T (2004) <u>Design sourcebook for Early Childhood</u>. Childspace New Zealand. Contact Mindstretchers in UK

Dimensions Foundation website - www.dimensionsfoundation.org

Goldschmied, E and Jackson,S (1994) <u>People under Three</u>. London. Routledge

Hannaford. C. (1977) <u>The Dominance Factor</u> Great Ocean Publishers

Hurst and Joseph (1998) <u>Supporting Early learning</u>, The way Forward   Open University Press

McLean (1991) The Human Encounter. Falmer Press

Nature World Forum website - www.worldforumfoundation.org

New Zealand Ministry of Education (1993) <u>Te Whariki</u> Wellington Learning Media Limited

<u>Norwegian Barneharge (2005)</u> - E.E.C.E.R.A. Conference 2006

Pahl. K. (1999) <u>Transformations</u> Meaning Making in Nursery Trentham Books

Roberts, R. (1995) <u>Self Esteem and successful Early Learning</u> London, Hodder and Stoughton

Scott (1996) in Nutbrown,C.(1996) <u>Chidren's Rights and Early Education</u>

SOEID (1999) <u>Curriculum framework for children 3-5</u> Edinburgh, The Scottish Office

Tizard & Hughes (1977) Staff b=Behaviour in Pre-School Centres JofEd Psych.18

Warden (2002) The Right To Be Me

Warden (2005) The Potential of a Puddle

Warden (2006) Talking & Thinking Floorbooks